Five States That Could Not Wait

Five States That Could Not Wait: Lessons for Health Reform from Florida, Hawaii, Minnesota, Oregon, and Vermont

Edited by Daniel M. Fox and John K. Iglehart

Health Affairs and Milbank Memorial Fund

Distributed by:
Blackwell Publishers
238 Main Street
Cambridge, Massachusetts 02142
USA

108 Cowley Road
Oxford OX4 1JF
UK

Library of Congress Catalog Card Number
94–078093
ISBN 1–55786–693–7 HB
ISBN 1–55786–607–4 PB
Typeset in 10 point Bodoni Book by Sans Serif, Ann Arbor, MI.
Printed in the United States of America.

TABLE OF CONTENTS

FOREWORD

The papers collected in this book exemplify purposes that are shared by *Health Affairs* and the Milbank Memorial Fund. Since the founding of *Health Affairs* in 1981, its overriding objective has been to serve as a multidisciplinary peer-reviewed journal dedicated to the serious exploration of domestic and international health policy issues. The Fund, now in its ninth decade, defines its mission as informing influential senior public and private decision makers about data and ways of thinking that can improve health policy.

Both organizations strive for neutrality in contemporary debates about health policy. *Health Affairs* and the Fund seek to remain above the philosophical fray by not embracing one particular ideology but instead serving as a forum for all relevant views.

We call attention, however, to the extraordinary agreement among people of very different partisan loyalties from diverse states that is revealed in the papers in this collection. Leaders in these states agree that the political will to enact health reform can be mobilized and that they have been successful to date because they have created and maintained broad coalitions.

The title of this book expresses the urgency and pride felt by the leaders of the five states. It was adapted from a statement about health reform by Florida Governor Lawton Chiles: "We just can't wait, given what the costs are."

Samuel L. Milbank
Chairman
Milbank Memorial Fund

William B. Walsh, M.D.
Publisher
Health Affairs

INTRODUCTION

The states are much more than laboratories of democracy, especially in health policy. State policy and politics matter enormously in how and if Americans have jobs and how they travel to them, how and where they are educated, and, of course, whether they have access to affordable health care.

As we write midway through 1994, it seems possible that Congress and the President will soon agree on policies to reform access to health care and to control its costs. Whatever measures become national law will, however, give the states important responsibilities to regulate, provide, and finance health services. Precisely how the states would function in a reformed health system is now being debated in Congress, the administration, and the media, within interest groups, and among governors and state legislators.

National policy should also take account of lessons from the states that took initiative in health reform—the states that could not wait. These states have solved the most difficult problem in health policy: how to mobilize political will in order to enact and implement reforms that give more people access to care and contain the growth of costs. Each state's solution to the political problems of health reform has necessarily been unique to the needs, values, and interests of its residents.

The six papers in this book describe the hard work of politics and policy-making in the first five states to enact health reform: Hawaii, Oregon, Minnesota, Vermont, and Florida. The first paper describes what leaders in these states believe they have achieved and their analysis of why they were able to enact reform. Harry Nelson, for many years a medical writer for the *Los Angeles Times*, wrote this essay after listening to state leaders talk to each other about what they did and conducting follow-up interviews with them.

The leaders who talked with Nelson welcomed into their states the political scientists who wrote the papers that follow his: Lawrence Brown, Howard Leichter, and Deane Neubauer. These leaders encouraged other legislators and executive branch officials to talk to the authors and to make documents available to them. Moreover, leaders in each state read and commented, often pungently, on drafts of both the summary paper and those on each state. The final versions of all six papers are, however, the work of their authors and of the two of us as editors.

Health Affairs and the Milbank Memorial Fund worked together in preparing these papers for publication. Our first joint effort was the essay on Oregon, which *Health Affairs* published in an earlier version in 1991. Because of the positive response to that essay, especially from readers who make policy, the Fund commissioned the papers on the other states. In November 1992 the Fund convened a meeting of leaders from the five states. The discussion at this meeting was the basis of Nelson's article. *Health Affairs* then published, in the summer of 1993, a paper on Florida; shorter versions of the papers on Hawaii, Minnesota, and Vermont; and an update on Oregon.

These papers describe health reform in the most innovative states to mid-1993, when President Clinton launched his campaign for national legislation. Two other states, Maryland and Washington, enacted and began to implement health reform in 1993. Several other states are likely to enact reform legislation before Congress acts on a national program.

As this collection of papers goes to press, leaders in the reforming states are working to maintain the gains they have achieved to date within a national health program. They are talking with each other and with their representatives in Congress about how to preserve state achievements while endorsing national health reforms. Many of the state-specific solutions to problems of access, coverage, and costs that are described in this book will surely be in place when experts and voters assess the achievements and failures of the Clinton administration.

Daniel M. Fox John K. Iglehart

The States That Could Not Wait: Lessons for Health Reform from Florida, Hawaii, Minnesota, Oregon, and Vermont

*Harry Nelson**

*This report is the collective work of the following state leaders: Florida, Douglas Cook, Arthur Grindle, Fred Jones; Hawaii, Bob Grossmann, John C. Lewin, Jim Shon; Maine, Charlene Rydell; Minnesota, Duane Benson, Linda Berglin, Lee Greenfield, Dave Gruenes, Curtis Johnson, Mary Jo O'Brien; Oregon, Michael Garland, Mark Gibson, Bob Shoemaker, Jean Thorne; Vermont, Jan Backus, Hamilton Davis, Paul Harrington, Anya Rader.

APPROACHES TOWARD SOLUTION

Here is an outline of what leaders of state health reform in the five states believe needs to be done:

Devise ways to achieve universal access to health care for the currently uninsured and uninsurable.

Take steps to control costs by:

- reforming the health insurance industry
- moving toward community rating
- cutting administrative costs by integrating state agencies that deal with health care and developing common billing requirements across all payers, public and private
- implementing controls to regulate high-cost technology
- changing the behaviors of providers and patients
- increasing the ratio of primary care physicians to specialists
- undertaking and applying research on the outcomes of particular treatments in order to use resources more efficiently
- encouraging preventive health services and managed care
- instituting practice guidelines for physicians
- reforming the tort system

Decide on the method of paying for universal access.

This glance at what the five states have accomplished to date will first describe what is unique for each state and then briefly list the highlights. For a more detailed outline, see Summary of Legislation, page 20.

HAWAII

As the only state that has actual experience with mandated, employment-based health insurance, Hawaii can show others how to make this approach work, de-

scribe its limits, and delineate the kinds of additional programs that are needed to extend services to everyone.

Employers are required to provide insurance for all workers spending more than twenty hours per week on the job.

Low-cost insurance is offered to persons with incomes below 300 percent of the poverty level through the State Health Insurance Program (SHIP), which subsidizes premiums on a sliding scale and strongly emphasizes illness prevention.

Together with Medicaid, SHIP covers about 93 percent of persons under age sixty-five.

OREGON

Oregon is the only state to build its approach on the notion that a priority list of health services could be used to define the basic package of guaranteed services.

Tax incentives have been created for small employers to help cover employees on a voluntary basis. If there are not enough enrollees by 1995, employers will be required to provide coverage to employees and their dependents or face being taxed and having their employees entered in a public plan.

All persons up to the poverty level will be covered by Medicaid.

All health care services for Medicaid, and eventually those contracted for by employers, will be ranked according to their effectiveness and other criteria, and the number of covered services will be determined by the legislature at least every two years based on available funding.

The Medicaid waiver needed for implementation of the plan was approved by the federal government in March 1993, with constraints the state can accept.

MINNESOTA

Minnesota is the state most dedicated to using practice guidelines and instituting a total expenditure cap to contain costs and to pay for universality through cost savings plus new taxes designated for health care.

The newly created MinnesotaCare Plan will be a major source of insurance coverage for low-income families and individuals. Eventually it will incorporate Medicaid and other indigent programs.

Insurance reform has been instituted as a step toward community rating. The law requires insurers to offer plans with minimum benefits and cost-sharing provisions to small employers, guarantee the issuance and renewability of coverage, and extend most of these provisions to the individual insurance market.

A commission has been created to develop a plan to reduce health care inflation by 10 percent per year for five years, beginning in 1993. The commission's first report, issued on schedule in January 1993, is now before the legislature for enactment of cost control under "competitive managed care."

The state has begun initiatives to increase the education and retention of primary care providers.

VERMONT

Vermont is unique in creating a clear, centralized body and process for defining the public choice between a single-payer system and a multipayer system. Its commitment to community rating makes Vermont an important state laboratory with which other states can compare their plans and results.

The Vermont Health Care Authority was created to design two alternative health care systems—a single-payer and a multipayer system—by November 1993. Both plans should offer universal coverage by October 1994, including provisions for global budgeting, uniform health benefits for all residents, centralized planning, incentives to contain costs, reimbursement mechanisms for providers, and recommendations for incorporating long-term care. This decision-making body has also been instructed to consider insurance reform and provisions for increasing the number of primary care physicians.

FLORIDA

Florida is unique in its commitment to a play-or-pay approach to universal access and to the formation of a state health services corps for improving geographic access.

A law has been enacted that guarantees access to health care for every resident by December 1994; the law also created the Agency for Health Care Administration, which, by December 1994, will consolidate health care financing, purchasing, and planning, and which will regulate health facilities and professionals as well as cost-containment functions. This agency will also be responsible for developing a Florida Health Plan, designed to provide private or public health insurance for all Floridians.

LESSONS TO BE LEARNED

Here are some of the essentials for success, say the leaders from the five states:

- Build on the strengths of existing programs because they can act as the foundation for further reform.
- Design a road map to where you want to go.
- Knowledgeable and dynamic leaders are a key to the success of health reforms.
- Develop the best cost-effective health care database.
- Examine carefully the single-payer system versus the multi-payer system in your state—and do not call it a Canadian system, even if you want one.
- Work with community groups in order to organize a large base of public support.
- Work with the news media.
- Remember that opposition groups are not monolithic. Exploit the splinter groups among the providers and within the insurance industry.
- Capitalize on disappointments.
- Build in a system to evaluate your progress so that you do not advance too far down the road to make corrections.
- Be sure that your legislation offers enough flexibility for the executive branch to maneuver to bring people together.
- Give your legislation firm implementation dates.

Here are illustrations from the five states of the most important of these steps.

Build on the strengths of existing programs because they can act as the foundation for further reform.

Insurance reform:

Legislation for insurance market reform has been introduced for several years in most of the fifty states.

Programs for children:

In *Vermont*, a 1988 expansion of coverage for poor children demonstrated that some opponents of universal care were beginning to accept the concept.

The passage of *Minnesota*'s plan is credited largely to a popular program for high-risk children that had been in place since 1976 and to a risk pool for "uninsurable" persons passed in 1988. The 1976 program is partly subsidized by a tax on insurance companies, thus providing a precedent.

Health Maintenance Organizations (HMOs):

Minnesota's reform efforts benefitted from the state's twenty-year history with managed care. Since 1973 Minnesota has mandated all employers of fifty or more workers that provide health insurance to offer an HMO as an option to their employees. Minnesota is now in the process of encouraging managed care in rural areas, where HMOs are weak, by forming networks of providers unaffiliated with HMOs.

A secondary benefit of HMOs in Minnesota emerged when the HMO lobby favored community rating and recommended that a provider tax be a source of financing of the reform bill.

Prenatal care:

In *Oregon*, the priority-setting process developed from budget decisions made after the legislature expanded prenatal care and other services for poor women and infants who previously had none, and discontinued funding for the most expensive organ transplants.

Employer mandates:

In *Hawaii*, the entire reform was built on the 1974 law that mandated all employers not covered by collective bargaining to provide health insurance for employees. Until the law was implemented, most legislators were unable to see existing gaps and propose ways to fill them.

Public input:

The formation in 1983 of a civic organization, *Oregon* Health Decisions, to solicit public input on health matters heralded an early rumbling of discontent with the system. Six years later, the organization became a vehicle for holding community meetings at which members of the public guided the setting of priorities for health services.

Medicaid:

Some of the strategies used to accomplish *Florida*'s 1992 reform package had their basis in a 1984 state law that made Florida the first state to impose a tax on net hospital operating revenues. The state used the money to create a trust fund to finance the expansion of the state's Medicaid and primary care services. During the 1992 session, legislators threatened to use the provider tax in order to win acceptance of its measures. The legislature also continued an earlier practice of appointing task forces to look into various health service problems and used their recommendations to strengthen support for reforms.

Design a road map to where you want to go.

One reason for reluctance to take on health reform is the magnitude of the required overhaul. Here is what happened in the five states:

Leaders in each state developed a big picture of the goals and elements of a mature, reformed system.

They identified the existing elements of their system that could be enhanced while moving toward reform.

They mapped out reforms step by step, building incrementally on each achievement in legislative content and political mobilization.

Initial success was possible in several of the states because interest groups did not perceive the approach of a major reform. For example, in *Hawaii*, few appreciated the implications of the prepaid health care act when it passed. Instead, most viewed it as a logical expansion of a set of benefits tailored to labor union pressures. Prepaid health care is now more than a labor issue.

Similarly, in *Oregon*, the list of health service priorities for Medicaid patients was not initially viewed as a way to define adequate care for everybody.

Knowledgeable and dynamic leaders are a key to the success of health reforms. Each of the five states can point to leaders who played a crucial role in their reform process.

In *Minnesota*, a group of seven legislators worked with the governor, setting aside partisan differences and dedicating themselves to the cause of health care reform. All seven legislators were experienced. Each held a key position in the house or senate. Four were Democrats, three were Republicans. Each was committed to accommodation rather than partisan politics, even in the face of the Republican governor's earlier veto of a health reform bill. The group's shared dedication to reform and its skillful leadership combined with the governor's subsequent support to defeat a barrage of opposition by medical organizations and hospitals.

In *Oregon*, the senate president led a coalition of key legislators from both houses, joined by the leadership of various interest groups. The senate president, a physician, was the dominant force in formulating the new health policy, partly because the governor had other priorities.

In *Hawaii*, the governor, who was interested in health, worked with legislative health committees chaired by individuals who were committed to health care improvements (but not tied to provider or payer interest groups). Their cooperation accounted for reform changes.

In *Vermont*, the governor, a physician, asserted leadership and was supported by key legislators in both houses.

In *Florida*, the governor, a former U.S. Senator who was keenly interested in maternal and child care issues, propelled the drive for health care reform. He appointed a task force to integrate the work of two earlier groups that had focused separately on private and public health responsibilities.

Develop the best cost-effective health care database.

Accurate data are an important aid to achieving universal access and cost containment. There is no shortage of data, but reliable data are hard to obtain. Insurance carriers, for example, can supply lots of statistics that do not add up to the whole story.

Minnesota used an actuary's information, but found it imprecise. Legislators had to make adjustments to the actuary's information, using data from HMOs.

In *Oregon*, data convinced legislators of the need for reform by defining the gaps in the system and revealing what kinds of care were unavailable to the uninsured.

People who do not want reform may use lack of data as an excuse to stall reform. The five states learned to use what they had. Each state then took steps to create a cost-effective data-gathering system that could collect relevant data from the private sector.

Examine carefully the single-payer system versus the multipayer system in your state—and do not call it a Canadian system, even if you want one.
Support for a Canadian type single-payer plan existed in most of the five states. However, single-payer supporters failed to command a strong role in influencing the legislation passed by any state. Yet the Vermont and Florida laws expressly state that a single-payer plan can be an option in the future; switching to a single payer is a possibility for any of the states if the first approach fails.

There are formidable barriers to state enactment of single-payer plans. For example, it may not be practical to abolish insurance companies, one aim of some single-payer plans. Moreover, if states did so, current federal law preempts their authority to reform the self-insured portion of the market, which accounts for about half of all insured workers. A single-payer system would have to be national, or at least it would require the lifting of federal constraints from the states.

In *Oregon*, the single-payer plan failed primarily because its promoters realized their bill would never pass the house, although it possibly could have passed the senate. Although unions supported the legislature's multipayer approach, they cautiously joined the multipayer coalition, believing such reform to be in the right direction and wishing to add their voices to single-payer arguments as the Oregon plan progressed.

Oregon legislators believe the first critical step is to make a statutory commitment to universal access. This commitment, they say, is essential to creating a comprehensive policy and building a structure within which a policy can operate effectively. Establishing that commitment was the primary goal of their health care reform.

They see the decision about how to pay for universal access as being secondary. The money collection methodology, the legislators say, can be determined on the basis of political feasibility. The legislators believed that consumers who prefer a single-payer approach would not argue against universal access merely because they dislike how it is paid for.

In *Vermont* in the early 1990s, antipoverty groups and unions were pressuring for coverage of the uninsured. Business was disturbed by increases in the cost of health insurance premiums. Everybody wanted reform. The issue was whether reform should be radical or mainstream. Unions, advocates for the poor, and the American Association of Retired Persons (AARP) pushed for a Canadian-style system. Just about everybody else wanted a multipayer plan.

Strong support for the single-payer bill bound together the diverse opposing forces and increased their willingness to support a multipayer bill. There was vocal support for a single-payer plan among the public, but hardly any in the legislature. The governor's view was that the single-payer bill offered no mechanism to pay for increased access. Legislators looked with disfavor upon single-payer advocates out of fear that the government would be the single payer, placing lawmakers in an uncomfortable position when money is scarce. A clause in the new law postpones until 1994 the legislature's decision to fund the program with a single- or multipayer system—or with a mix of both.

In *Minnesota*, a single-payer bill was blocked by the powerful state senate health committee, which declined to go any further than a commission's recommendation to retain mainstream payment methods.

Florida's experience with a single-payer also was short lived. The introduction of a single payer bill in 1988 aroused alarm in the state's business community and sparked the creation of two task forces that recommended spearheading the multipayer plan, which was passed and signed into law by the governor in 1992.

Work with community groups in order to organize a large base of public support.

State officials reported that they increased public support for their initiatives by taking the following actions:

They gained commitments from persons and groups for more than a short-term effort. They defined "success" in terms of years, not months.

They recruited unions early and especially tried to minimize threats to civil service workers.

They sought out elements of political parties and factions that had some interest in reform.

They contracted with a nonprofit organization to hold meetings for the purpose of informing the public of the intent of health reform and explaining its necessity.

Work with the news media.

The public does not respond well to statistics, but it does to stories. *Minnesota* provides an example.

In 1991, when reform-minded legislators in Minnesota began building their case, they were aided by the Children's Defense Fund (CDF), which found patients with serious untreated health problems. CDF prepared press releases describing these cases and sent one each day to legislators and to the press. The stories appeared daily during the crucial period when legislators were negotiating their health reform bills and helped to create public support. Earlier, when a cost commission was working on recommendations that were to form the backbone of the legislation, heavy news coverage helped build public support (60 percent, said the polls) for a tax increase to cover the uninsured.

In *Oregon*, the publicity resulting from the death of a seven-year-old boy set the stage for discussion of health care rationing. The legislature shifted funding for organ transplants from the regular Medicaid budget to an optional list, which meant that requests for transplants had to compete with mental health and other social programs. Funding for transplants was not included in the final budget. The case of the seven-year-old boy, whose only insurance was Medicaid, received national attention when the state refused to pay for his transplant. Private contributions were insufficient to pay for the surgery and the boy died.

Remember that opposition groups are not monolithic. Exploit the splinter groups among the providers and within the insurance industry.

The degree of opposition to proposed legislation by organized medicine, hospitals, and insurers varied from state to state. The *Oregon* and *Vermont* medical and hospital associations, unlike those in Minnesota and Florida, supported reforms early in the political process.

Physicians played important roles as legislators or officials in Oregon and in Vermont. In Oregon, the legislative sponsor of the reform package was an emergency room physician who dominated the reform. Medical societies did not speak for all the physicians. Many primary care providers, especially those who worked in clinics and health centers, differed with official medical opinion.

Here are some examples. First, providers:

When *Vermont*'s governor died in 1991, the new governor, a physician, announced his support for the reform bill. He is credited with providing level-headed guidance, which helped to deflect the opposition of organized medicine without seriously damaging the bill's intent.

Vermont doctors wanted change. But they believed that everybody, including the public, must share the burden of cost containment. They wanted to participate actively on the legislation's proposed boards, which would decide on prices and budgets. They were concerned about limitations on clinical freedom. They also wanted quicker resolution of malpractice claims. Given these demands, they supported the bill.

The Vermont Hospital Association supported the general direction of the multipayer bill and worked closely with the legislators to ensure that cost containment did not fall too heavily on hospitals.

In *Florida*, the chief opponent of reform was the state medical association. Florida physicians have substantial stakes in expensively equipped diagnostic centers and other businesses to which they make referrals. The state is well stocked with for-profit hospitals and, in some counties, with excessive amounts of high-tech equipment.

Organized medicine failed in its efforts to kill reform because it had exhausted its energies in an unsuccessful fight to defeat legislation (unrelated to the reform bills) that barred physicians from making referrals to facilities in which they had financial interest.

The *Minnesota* Medical Association (MMA) worked hard to arouse the public against reform. It was especially disturbed by the 2 percent provider tax. The Mayo Clinic and other high-visibility institutions joined forces against it. Since passage of the bill, both the MMA and Mayo have supported the changes and are cooperating with the commission.

Not all provider groups opposed reform. Support came from family practitioners, HMOs, and the state's nurses, psychologists, chiropractors, public health workers, mental health professionals, and community health clinics.

The seven key legislators and the governor, who set aside partisan differences to achieve reform, agreed to adopt a policy that would prevent lobbyists from using a "divide and conquer" strategy.

For four months the seven legislators held secret meetings at which no formal votes were taken. All seven had to agree on every decision made. The group identified what were to be the essential elements of their bill.

When the first bill was drafted in Minnesota, the hospitals and organized medicine were surprised by the fact that the two parties had secretly worked out these compromises. Instead of suggesting constructive changes, organized medicine, hospitals, and high-tech medical equipment firms launched an aggressive opposition campaign.

A critical difference involved the choice between a provider tax or an income-tax surcharge to pay for the new insurance coverage. The provider tax won out. The bill passed despite powerful opposition because the tactics used by opponents of the bill antagonized legislators and solidified their resolve to institute reforms.

And some examples about insurers:

In *Vermont*, the bitterest opponent of reform legislation was the insurance industry—but not all insurers. Blue Cross/Blue Shield was losing money and was eager for reform. Some large commercial companies did not entirely agree with their smaller allies.

The scene had been set in 1991 when the state's eighty insurance companies suffered a sharp defeat because they were forced to offer community rates for the small group market. In 1992 they faced the prospect of having to extend community rating to the nongroup market, which the Blues were already doing.

Some of the insurance companies threatened to quit the state if the bill passed, while predicting that premium rates for the young would more than double and that the ranks of the uninsured would soar.

The new bill provided a safety net in case some carriers left the state. It also limited any premium rate increase to 20 percent per year, provided the company had a loss ratio (how much paid out in claims relative to premiums) of at least 70 percent. The loss rate for the Blues was high, but it was relatively low for the ten carriers writing nongroup policies.

The legislators did not compromise with the insurers. The bill passed and was signed by the governor.

Several carriers did leave the state and others have stopped taking new subscribers. The governor said he was disappointed that more did not leave.

In the beginning, the only opponents to the *Oregon* plan were small businesses. By 1991, however, a section of the insurance industry actively opposed certain elements of small group insurance reform proposals.

Small business in Oregon, as in most other states, objected that expanding coverage to 280,000 workers and dependents would cause many smaller concerns to fail. Legislators responded by enacting target voluntary subscription rates for working individuals who were currently uncovered and by continuing low-cost insurance coupled with income tax credits. They agreed to cancel the mandate if virtually all small business employees and their dependents were covered on a voluntary basis.

During the 1991 session, a segment of the insurance industry that serves small groups in Oregon became alarmed when legislators began reforms requiring insurers to grant coverage to all small groups. Their opposition centered on the community rating aspects of insurance reform. They were isolated politically, especially after the major insurance companies sided with the legislature because they saw an opportunity to level the marketplace.

In *Minnesota*, Democrats wanted to move to community rating and to apply controls on insurers that would prevent them from either denying coverage to persons with prior health conditions or reissuing policies.

The Republicans wanted to soften these goals by setting age brackets to lessen the premium increases that community rating would exact from young, healthy individuals.

The Blues and HMOs in general supported the Democrats' goals.

A chief concern of the Republicans was that the conditions created by insurance reform would cause the young and healthy to opt out of the health system. They also feared that the provider tax and other reforms opposed by organized medicine would cause physicians to leave the state.

With the controls now in effect, it should be possible to tell within a year whether the Republicans were correct.

Capitalize on disappointments.

In 1991, *Minnesota*'s governor vetoed a reform bill that would have restructured the health insurance system. However, less than a year later, HealthRight, an even broader reform, was enacted with the governor's blessing. The public wanted it, the governor apparently needed a political boost, and in 1992 the entire legislature was up for election.

The earlier experience hardened resolve and sharpened legislative talents, familiarized everybody with the problems, and gave proponents a better understanding of what they had to do to win.

When *Oregon*'s request for a federal waiver was turned down in August

1992, state officials responded with renewed vigor by submitting a revised request that was approved in March 1993.

THE TIME FOR ACTION

The difficulties of the legislative process and the complexities of health care reform might make the task seem impossible to many policy makers. However, leaders in the reforming states agree that the future for health reform is bright.

This brief outline of the experiences of five states demonstrates that significant health care reform can occur in this country and that the states have a central role in defining what is possible and practical. It shows also that health reform is an issue that now transcends the usual political dynamic and produces bipartisan leadership and a partnership between the executive and legislative branches of government.

Much tough work is ahead. Universal coverage and cost containment have not yet been realized in any state. Obstacles like federal preemption of state regulation of employee benefit plans must still be faced. Coalitions could dissolve. Key leaders and committee chairmen could be replaced. Future implementation dates could be bypassed.

But the people whose experiences are summarized in this report believe that the goals will be achieved if vision, leadership, and coalition building make it happen. Each state offers instructive experiences and potential resources. State action on health care reform can address fundamental concerns of Americans. It can also serve as a catalyst or a model for change at the federal level.

SUMMARY OF LEGISLATION

Following are profiles of steps toward health reform legislated by the five states. Each state built on earlier efforts and in every one the multiple barriers of partisan disagreement, interest group pressures, public skepticism, and exhausting meetings were faced and overcome. There were compromises. No victory was total. Gaps still exist. All five states are considering actions in the next legislative session to fill the gaps.

HAWAII

1974. The Prepaid Health Care Act, which covers all full-time employees, was passed. Half of the coverage is funded by the employer and half by the employee, except that the employee's share cannot exceed 1.5 percent of his or her total wages. A federal Medicaid waiver was successfully obtained.

A generous Medicaid program has been built in over the years since 1966.

1989. A State Health Insurance Program (SHIP) was created for groups not covered either by Medicaid or by prepaid health care. The state subsidized the program with sliding fees for the insured. For persons under 100 percent of poverty level, the plan is free.

1991. A Primary Care Network Bill was passed to develop primary health care centers throughout the state. A related bill offered incentives for medical schools to turn out more primary care doctors.

1991. Blue Ribbon Panel recommendations focused on administrative procedures, which included electronic claims processing, automated record keeping, a universal claims form, and improved data collection.

State subsidies were given to nonprofit agencies in areas such as mental health, preventive services, primary care, AIDS, teen health, and sex abuse counseling.

1992. A proposal to finance long-term-care insurance (requires a waiver from federal government).

Remaining gaps: Hawaii does not regulate health insurance, hospitals, doctors, or pharmacies. The health system has not yet "captured" the hardest-to-reach uninsured like the homeless, the mentally ill, immigrants and native Hawaiians. The mortality rate of the latter group is double that of the rest of the population.

OREGON

1983. Oregon Health Decisions (OHD), a nonprofit educational organization was formed and proceeded to hold community meetings and to issue recommendations on plans for the uninsured. OHD also increased public acceptance of the necessity for reform.

1987. The Oregon Department of Human Resources requested $2.2 million from the legislature to cover thirty-four organ transplants, a $1 million increase over the previous two years. State house and senate committees instead shifted transplants out of the regular budget and onto an optional priority list, where requests competed with mental health programs and head injury patients for funding.

1988. A proposal to appropriate $220,000 to fund five Medicaid transplants was defeated on grounds of "inequity" because 400,000 working Oregonians had no health insurance and were not eligible for Medicaid.

1989. Three new laws took effect over various time periods that made everyone below the federal poverty level eligible for Medicaid, eventually eliminating the uninsured status of 120,000 persons; providers were to be paid according to fees established by an independent actuary; access for 2,800 uninsurables was expanded by creating high-risk insurance pool coverage to an additional 260,000 employed persons. The level of care was to match Medicaid, which included high-cost procedures like transplants. Tax credits encouraged employers to cover employees. Some facets depended on federal waiver approval.

1990. The Health Services Commission and Oregon Health Decisions held fifty-eight public meetings and conducted a telephone survey to study citizens' values and preferences for medical/health situations and treatments.

1991. The Health Services Commission publicized a list of 709 health services and treatments arranged in order of priority for Medicaid funding. Available funding each year will determine how far down the list services will extend.

1991. The legislature reformed small group health insurance to require that all sales to small group insurers include the offer of a policy substantially similar to the Medicaid prioritized list.

1991. The Health Resources Commission was created to grapple with cost containment.

August 1992. The federal waiver required for Oregon to make changes in Medicaid was denied by the U.S. Secretary of Health and Human Services on the grounds that the plan was in conflict with the Americans with Disabilities Act.

November 1992. Oregon resubmitted a modified request for a waiver with a revised list of 688 condition/treatment pairs.

December 1992. The legislative committee determined that the Medicaid budget for 1993-95 will cut off services after number 568 out of 688 health services/treatments on the priority list.

March 1993. The federal waiver was approved for the revised plan.

Remaining gaps: It has not yet been determined either how the plan will contain costs or how expanded access will be funded. The governor has recommended a 1 percent tax on provider income.

MINNESOTA

1972. The state received a head start in managed care by mandating all employers of fifty or more insured workers to offer HMOs as an option.

1988. The Children's Health Plan was created for non-Medicaid, low-income pregnant women and children under six years of age. Funded by a minimum annual fee and a one-cent cigarette tax, it was expanded in 1991 to include all children through age eighteen.

1989-91. The Health Care Access Commission was formed and issued a report that contained far-reaching recommendations for reform, identified the uninsured, and suggested a twenty-five dollar annual fee per child. Its report provided the basis for the Minnesota Health Care Plan that the legislature passed by a comfortable margin in May 1991. The governor vetoed that bill.

1992. The Minnesota Health Care Plan was the basis for the HealthRight Law (now called Minnesota Care), which was passed and signed in April.

The law took a regulatory approach to containing costs, expanding access, reforming health insurance, dealing with rural health problems, collecting health care data, and finding ways to fund expanded access to health services. Funding will be achieved by a five-cent increase in the cigarette tax; a 2 percent hospital tax on gross patient revenues beginning in January 1993; a 2 percent tax on provider gross revenues beginning in January 1994; and a 1 percent tax beginning in 1996 on gross premiums for nonprofit health service plans and HMOs.

A Health Care Cost Containment Commission was created to set a target for slowing health cost inflation by 10 percent per year beginning in 1993; to establish statewide and regional goals on total spending; to foster regional health care planning; to restrain providers by retroactive monitoring of expenditures for high-tech items costing more than $500,000; to review the effects of treatment methods; to encourage health promotion; and to prohibit insurance companies from denying coverage to small businesses or refusing group policy renewals.

A Rural Health Advisory Council will be created to provide state aid to rural hospitals in trouble and loan forgiveness to rural doctors. The university of Minnesota will take steps to increase the number of primary care doctors and to reduce the number of specialists.

Gaps: The plan will cover only about 40 percent of the uninsured by 1997. Health insurance underwriting practices are not strictly regulated. Control over high technology may not be effective.

VERMONT

1987. The Vermont Health Insurance Plan was enacted to find ways to extend coverage to the uninsured. However, the governor and the assembly were unwilling to produce the $32 million required to provide comprehensive benefits to the state's 32,000 uninsured. Although it did not become law, the plan alerted the public, providers, business, and insurance companies to the need for universal coverage.

1992. The Vermont Health Care Reform Act became law. Its timetable extends through 1994 and it expands access for all children, institutes community rating for individual insurance policies, establishes a system of global budgeting, creates a Vermont Health Care Authority that is mandated to control costs and expand access, and sets a plan for the University of Vermont to train more primary care doctors.

In November *1993* the new three-member Health Care Authority Board must submit two universal access plans: one of these is to be a single payer and the second, a multipayer plan.

In January *1994* the General Assembly will meet to consider the Health Care Authority Board's proposals. If the legislature adopts a plan for universal access, a medical malpractice reform will begin. Regardless of whether a universal access plan is adopted, the board will establish annual unified health care budgets (global budgets) that set total spending levels on health care. Spending caps will be applied to hospitals only.

FLORIDA

1988. A single-payer plan bill was introduced with the backing of a national physicians' organization and senior citizens.

1990. The legislature and the governor created two task forces to survey the private and public health sectors and to make recommendations for change.

1991. The task forces decided on a "play or pay" type plan.

1992. The governor signed the Health Care Reform Act, which integrates the regulation and administration of the health industry and guarantees access to health care for every resident by 31 December 1994.

The act created the Agency for Health Care Administration (AHCA), which will consolidate health care financing, purchasing, and planning over a two-year period. It will also regulate health facilities and health professionals and oversee cost containment functions. The agency will include an eleven-member health care board, appointed by the governor, consisting of four providers, three representatives of businesses, one insurer, and three consumers.

AHCA will assume responsibility for issuing certificates of need, licensure, and certification, for overseeing health policy, and for regulating health facility costs.

By December 1994 the agency will be responsible for Medicaid and for developing the Florida Health Plan, which will provide private or public health insurance for all Floridians.

The agency also will be charged with reforming health insurance, limiting health care cost increases to manageable levels, restructuring health regulation, and establishing a health care database.

The guidelines for the Florida Health Plan include:

- Ensuring access to affordable basic benefits for all residents, regardless of health condition or employment status.
- Instituting cost containment by promoting preventive care and controlling proliferation of tertiary care; establishing practice guidelines and utilization systems; consolidating state health insurance programs; simplifying billing and administrative overhead; improving the system for handling medical negligence disputes.
- Instituting health insurance reforms.
- Establishing a comprehensive health data system for providers, facilities, and insurers.

The act creates a Florida Health Services Corps to encourage medical professionals to practice in underserved.

Commissions, Clubs, and Consensus: Reform in Florida

Lawrence D. Brown

As pressures for health care reform began to intensify in the mid-1980s, devotees of devolution would have been hard-pressed to argue that the states were a credible source of leadership. Sensing that bold efforts to repair the system would antagonize powerful provider and payer groups without yielding commensurate gratitude in the electorate, most state leaders lacked the political will to enter the fray. Constrained by pledges of "no new taxes" and pressured by myriad spending arenas in addition to health, states also lacked the fiscal capacity to subsidize the quest for universal coverage. Reform leadership, many concluded at the time, would come from Washington or not at all.

By 1990 the potential for state-initiated health reform looked very different. In 1988 Massachusetts became the first state to legislate a statewide play-or-pay plan. (Hawaii had enacted employer mandates, with no "pay" option, in 1974.) In 1989 Oregon won headlines with its plan to ration ("prioritize") health procedures for part of the Medicaid population and then to use that list of covered services as a minimum benefit package binding on employers. In the early 1990s Minnesota, Vermont, Washington, and Florida joined the ranks of states with legislation designed to move toward universal coverage, and many more states had such measures under earnest discussion. The states had by no means solved the problem of fiscal capacity, but clearly the earlier negative verdict on their political will had been exaggerated and premature.

As might be expected—and presumably desired—in the laboratory of federalism, the states leading the charge for change differ considerably in their preferred strategies and in the routes by which they reached them. This paper examines one of the most intriguing innovators, Florida, which in March 1992 created an Agency for Health Care Administration (AHCA) as a means explicitly expected to achieve affordable universal coverage for all Floridians by the end of 1994. In essence, Florida set off to find a consensus on the substantive problems of cost and access only to discover that none existed and that no one was sure what to do next. Convinced that fragmentation of public authority in the health policy sphere both defeated coherent control of the larger system and impaired the best efforts of the principal players—public and private—to hold a sensible, sustained discussion about reform, Florida has put its faith in reorganization. The hope is that a rational administrative structure that brings all (or most) of the players in the financing and regulatory games within a common organizational framework, in an agency that works under a skillful director who reports to the governor and stands accountable to the legislature, is a necessary—and perhaps even sufficient—condition for building agreement on reformist means and ends. This paper tries to explain how Florida came to enter the class of leading state health policy innovators and why it embraced the approach that it did.

AN EARLY INNOVATOR

Judged by surface data and impressions, Florida is an improbable source of "progressive" health policy departures. Despite strong liberal enclaves in and around Miami, much of the state is rural, Southern, and politically and culturally conservative. Lacking a personal income tax, and tenaciously committed to that omission as a spur to the growth on which it relies for revenues, Florida tends to rank "near the bottom of the states in almost every indicator of government effort."[1] The state has long displayed the usual package of problems of poorer southern states: high rates of infant mortality and low-birthweight babies, low Medicaid eligibility (24 percent of federal poverty in 1984, 31 percent today), and low rates of payment and provider participation in Medicaid. Gaps in private-sector coverage mirror the public. Ninety-five percent of Florida firms employ fewer than twenty-five people.[2] Also, much of the economy depends on agriculture, construction, tourism, and other service industries that often fail to cover their workers. In consequence, 18.5 percent of Florida's population—and fully 22.9 percent of its nonaged citizens—lack health insurance.[3] The very magnitude of the problem seems itself to inhibit innovation: For example, Hawaii, Massachusetts, and Minnesota had about half of Florida's percentage of uninsured population when they moved toward universal coverage.

Appearances can deceive, however: Florida was one of the first and boldest innovators in state health policy. The pattern commenced in 1984, when Florida enacted the nation's first state-based revenue assessment ("sick tax") on hospitals, to create a trust fund to finance the expansion of Medicaid and primary care services. The visible deficiencies of Medicaid and the tribulations of the uninsured were significant stimuli to action, but those familiar features of the federalist scene do not explain why, much less how, Florida chose to pioneer a new funding strategy for the poor. A fuller explanation requires a look at particular features of Florida's health policies and how political leaders chose to manage them.

Roots of reform. In the early 1980s both the organized elderly and business coalitions were ardently petitioning the legislature for relief from rising health costs; both targeted hospital spending as the logical locus of intervention. Competition was in the air, but few knew what it meant concretely, and those who were not seduced by its allure countered by pressing the case for tough rate regulation of hospitals. Meanwhile, about 40 percent of Florida's hospitals had become for-profit, generating behavior patterns that had fans of competition and regulation alike crying out for a leveling of the playing field. The for-profits were allegedly shirking their fair share of the state's sizable burden of uncompensated care. An observer recalled in an interview that "a two-class system of care was developing and everyone knew it. The for-profits would give the uninsured guy who showed up in the ER fifteen dollars for a taxi and send him to the nearest public hospital." In a potent and unusual split within "the industry," the voluntary and public hospitals pressed their common case for fiscal relief.

Three-part strategy. As state leaders sought to reconcile these diverse concerns, they devised a three-part strategy that served them well in the early 1980s and again a decade later. First, they appointed commissions to explore problems, canvass solutions, and—probably most important—educate dozens of prominent public and private players about what might be done and who wanted what. In 1981 a task force headed by former state legislator Buddy Mackay set the stage by pondering competitive and regulatory issues. Then in 1983 the Task Force on Competition and Consumer Choice, headed by former state senator Bob McKnight, began drafting "a blue print for state-wide policy changes."[4] The group became a central focus for group presentations, for ventilation of issues before the press and the public, and, in time, for legislative recommendations.

Second, political leaders adroitly wielded policy "clubs"—the threat of firm intervention that groups wanted to avoid—to win acceptance of more modest measures. As the field-leveling revenue assessment began to gather support, the for-profit hospitals threatened to try to block it. Legislators responded by swinging the (credible) club of a hospital rate-setting system and thus got the revenue assessment plan back on track.[5] Third, clubs notwithstanding, Florida policymakers assumed that workable reforms required complex bargains that blended benefits with costs in ways that gave all major participants some victory to take away from the table. In 1986 Gary J. Clarke (now the state's director of Medicaid and an important figure in the 1992 reforms) captured well a political style that worked in 1984 and recurred in 1992:

> The provisions of the law reflect both the comprehensive nature of the approach as well as the compromises and consensus of all concerned. Businesses were assured an upper limit on hospital cost increases but were left free to negotiate their own best deals with hospitals. Hospitals escaped the dreaded burdens of either full-fledged budget/rate regulation or mandated charity care requirements. Voluntary hospitals, and especially public hospitals, were guaranteed that their increased burden of Medicaid care would be relieved in direct proportion to the amount of such care they provide—more than offsetting the increased tax to which they were subjected. Advocates for the poor and Medicaid program expansion were able to increase overall revenue by at least a third, without resorting to any apparent increase in direct citizen taxation (sales or income tax). And issues that were too complicated or for which there was insufficient time were left for further study. As the 38 to 0 and 112 to 0 votes in the Senate and House respectively demonstrate, the hard-fought program was in the end supported by all interested parties in the state, and most legislators and lobbyists (except those from some individual hospitals) left the capital that spring well-pleased with their efforts.[6]

The Health Care Access Act of 1984 created (among other provisions) a Public Medical Assistance Trust Fund initially sustained by a tax of 1 percent of net hospital operating revenues (rising to 1.5 percent in subsequent years). At the state's Medicaid federal matching rate of 56 percent, Florida envisioned about $200 million annually of new monies with which to expand and improve Medicaid and enhance primary care.[7]

COMMISSIONS CONTINUED: MOVING BEYOND MEDICAID

As the 1980s advanced, it became clear to most health care leaders in Florida that extra hospital-derived revenues to expand Medicaid and primary care services were but a modest first step toward effective reform of a system that staggered under multiple burdens. After an early spell of confusion in which new Medicaid enrollments, and drawdowns on the new trust fund, were much smaller and slower than anticipated, the innovations of 1984 did enable the state to improve markedly its payments to hospitals and physicians. But simultaneous developments reduced this progress to a drop in the bucket. Trust fund–assisted payments to Medicaid providers increased, but between 1985 and 1991 the program's enrollment doubled, and overall spending soared.

The increases reflected some fairly intractable trends: The recession swelled the ranks of the unemployed, the uninsured, and those on welfare; federal mandates added new groups to the program; immigration to Florida swelled; and various pathologies (acquired immunodeficiency syndrome [AIDS], drug abuse, mental illness, and others) got medicalized and "Medicaidized," driving up utilization. Meanwhile, Florida continued to add jobs in sectors that typically did not extend health coverage to workers; Medicare (and Medicaid) shifted costs more aggressively as their fiscal worries worsened; business watched its health spending grow and cried for help; the numbers of elderly in Florida and their anxiety about the rising costs of care increased; uncompensated care grew more burdensome, the trust fund notwithstanding; and suspicions about unnecessary treatments and other sources of waste in the system deepened. By the end of the decade voices rose in every corner of the system and the state urging state policymakers to propose solutions.

Some of these pressures were aggravated by Florida's demographics and economic infrastructure, but none was unique to the state; as in 1984, these insistent sources of demand for change did not, themselves, explain the state's capacity to supply it. An adequate answer lies again in the realms of political choice and conflict management, and its first element is (again) the state's creative use of commissions to set a reform agenda.

In July 1989 the Florida legislature created two multimember task forces—one on Private-Sector Health Care Responsibilities, the other on Government-Financed Health Care—and instructed them to report their findings by March 1991.[8] Over nearly two years the two groups held meetings and worked to forge agreement on the nature of the problems and preferred avenues for change among a wide range of interests. Not surprisingly, the two converged rather closely in their indictment of the usual suspects for the system's problems: unhealthy lifestyles, excessive utilization, cost shifting, insurers' preferred risk selection, and more. The two also seemed to be in harmony on a broad division of labor in the public/private partnership: The public sector should secure cost containment and coverage for the unemployed, and the private sector should contrive to insure all its workers. There was also significant agreement on general strategic directions. Both embraced extensive reform of health insurance practices, the promotion of prevention and primary care, and hard choices about what basic benefits public and private insurers should be expected to cover.

In three respects, however, the public-sector group sketched an agenda with sharper policy teeth and more visible political sponsorship than did its private-sector counterpart. First, the Task Force on Government-Financed Health Care boldly proposed ambitious goals with short time horizons. It flatly recommended that (1) all citizens of the state should enjoy universal access, meaning "readily available access to primary care and a means of paying for that care;" (2) 95 percent of employees and dependents should have primary care coverage, or employer mandates should be adopted; and (3) per capita health care costs should increase by no more than the overall rate of inflation—and all this by 1996.[9]

Second, the public-sector group's willingness to cut to the chase by 1996 came accompanied by a blunt prescription about how to make the cut: "A single state agency, either existing or to be established, shall be given responsibility for the reform of the health care system."[10] The importance of this recommendation may be gauged by the insistence of eight of the group's seventeen members (including all three of its hospital representatives) on filing dissenting views and opinions blasting it.[11] Third, the public-sector task force's vision of bold goals, tight time lines, and concentrated public authority became identified with its chairman, C. Fred Jones, a widely respected veteran Democratic legislator from central Florida and a conservative. Jones's standing assured that when he talked about the need for an "800-pound gorilla—someone to sit all you interests down to get your attention and get you to negotiate in good faith"—a broad audience within the public and private sectors and within the liberal and conservative camps took respectful notice.[12]

As early facilitators of change, the task forces had worked well. The systemic nature and multiple elements of the problems had been laid out for all to see. A broad range of interest-group leaders had received a two-year education in policy pros and cons and in the values and interests of their task force colleagues, and had been equipped to argue the case for change within their various sectors. The urgency and legitimacy of a continuing quest by both the public and private sectors for reforms had been established. Some pointed and controversial suggestions about what to do here and now had entered the public and private agendas. The challenge now was to turn up the heat—to move those suggestions (or substitutes for them) higher on those agendas and closer to legislative enactment.

THE CANADIAN CLUB: LEGISLATIVE MOMENTUM FROM MIAMI

Florida is a southern conservative state with a major twist: the presence of sizable numbers of seniors, often emigrés from the Northeast and Midwest, many of whom bring and retain liberal, activist expectations of government that distinguish them from younger, more conservative Floridians. Especially salient and cohesive is the concentration of liberal Democratic, largely Jewish ex-New Yorkers in and around Miami and Miami Beach. From one perspective (for instance, that of the uninsured), Medicare coverage should make these seniors some of the health care system's most satisfied customers. From another viewpoint (their own), however, they too are hapless victims of the system: Muddling through on fixed incomes, they watch out-of-pocket medical costs and Medigap premiums soar, and any protracted demand for long-term care could exhaust their assets. Many seniors, therefore, tune in assiduously to the debates about health care reform and expect (probably wrongly) that change will mean lower medical costs for them as well as for the uninsured and the working insured. In pondering reform, this group, many of whom formed their political attitudes in the New Deal era, tend to be more accepting of government-centered solutions than are younger cohorts. The mention of single-payer, Canadian-style schemes strikes no fear in their hearts. Quite the contrary, they—like the national American Association of Retired Persons (AARP), whose "line" they generally echo—profess not to understand why the U.S. government should not assign itself a leading role in securing affordable universal coverage, and insistently press the question, "Why can't we have a health system as good as the Canadians have?"

These liberal views found practical expression in 1988 (and thereafter) with the introduction of House Bill (HB) 1, the Florida Universal Health Access Plan, by Rep. Elaine Gordon of North Miami. The bill, strongly backed by the AARP, would give Florida a Canadian-style plan, that is, a publicly financed, single-payer system without employer mandates, copayments, or deductibles. A commission would set statewide global budgets for all providers, negotiate fee schedules with providers within the global budget limits, and set fair premiums for comprehensive benefits.[13] The bill had little short-term prospect for passage. But, precisely because its potential political appeal (should more incremental alternatives falter) was unknown, it tossed a weighty gauntlet before other legislators. If they truly favored reform but would not endorse Gordon's Canadian-inspired version, what better ideas might they care to offer? HB 1 was, in short, a potent club that providers and policymakers could not ignore. Gordon herself called it "a two-by-four between the eyes of the system."

In 1991 a prominent Miami Beach liberal, Rep. Mike Abrams, offered a promising alternative. Abrams would establish a public utility–style commission to canvass reform alternatives—a single-payer system would be one among several—and to propose detailed plans for a major overhaul of the system. This approach appealed to both Dade County liberals and conservatives who thought it a reasonable facsimile of Jones's 800-pound gorilla.

A participant later described in an interview the political alignment emerging in support of reform. Business, alarmed at health care spending, could perhaps be persuaded to endorse mandates so long as they followed a decent interval of voluntary efforts to expand coverage and were attached to firm government assurance of cost containment. The hospitals remained skeptical of consolidated government controls but might wax lukewarm if physicians were tightly regulated too. The Department of Health and Rehabilitative Services was even prepared to yield some health functions to the proposed commission.

This skittish coalition carried the commission bill through the solidly Democratic House, but the Senate, where Democrats held a narrow 21–19 majority, then balked. Governor Lawton Chiles, newly installed in office and still composing his health reform agenda, did not fight for the bill, while the Florida Medical Association (FMA), fearful of what a commission might do to physician incomes and practice patterns, opposed it aggressively and successfully.

From the ashes of the commission bill in 1991 rose a clear and increasingly hopeful prognosis for the next round. If business stayed in the reform fold, the main challenges were, first, to split provider opposition by enticing the ambivalent hospitals to the side of change and, second, to convince Governor Chiles to throw his formidable political weight into the struggle. The hospitals were remarkably obliging. A spokesman recalled a soul-searching retreat in 1991 from which the nonprofit and public hospitals emerged with a new dedication to reform. The 1991 legislative session had produced results that hospitals did not like. But, the spokesman said, "It made us rethink our position. The system was broken, it needs fixing, the legislature would continue to pursue change. We saw that we'd better be proactive." Their reappraisal cleared the strategic field. Now, if the governor came out swinging, the physician lobby might be isolated and quite possibly overcome.

CRAFTING CONSENSUS: ALONG COMES CHILES

In most states major health reforms are difficult to achieve in the legislature alone, which is usually riven by factions and limited in the scope and powers of its leadership. Generally, strong executive commitment to and participation in major policy departures are essential to their progress, and in this respect Florida was no exception. When Governor Chiles joined the search for policy reforms, the prospects for a happy legislative outcome increased markedly.

In 1990 Chiles, a veteran of eighteen years as a Democrat in the U.S. Senate, wrested the Florida governor's office from incumbent Bob Martinez, a Republican who had largely stayed on the sidelines of health reform. While in Washington Chiles had paid sustained attention to maternal and child health issues but had not joined the swelling ranks of self-proclaimed "health leaders." Once he settled into Tallahassee, however, health reform quickly shot to the top of his agenda, for reasons much like those driving other governors.

Entering office with big plans for improving Florida's physical infrastructure and social services, Chiles quickly discovered that health care was eating up most of the money he hoped to use for his varied priorities; that is, projected growth in Medicaid spending consumed much of the estimated growth in the state's public revenues. Meanwhile, the recession, immigration, cost shifting, the growth of the uninsured population, and other factors were pushing the program's enrollment and costs ever higher, with no relief in view. Something had to be done, and because Medicaid costs were in so many ways driven from without, internal repairs to the program would not suffice. Decrying the "outrageous cycle" and the fiscal and political "mess" it produced, Chiles appointed a twenty-one-member health care working group and told it to return with recommendations within three months.

The governor's situational commitment to reform gained extra force and urgency when he attended a meeting of the National Governors' Association (NGA) in Seattle and joined a debate about the hows and whens of universal coverage. The assembled chief executives were debating a resolution that exhorted the nation to achieve universal coverage by the year 2000. Proposing an amendment to the measure, Chiles eloquently argued that the goal could not wait that long. For one thing, rising costs would demolish state budgets well before that deadline; for another, postponing universal coverage into the tenure of incumbents' political successors was no profile in courage. The NGA might do as it pleased, declared Chiles, but he for one was determined to see universal coverage achieved in Florida before the end of his current term in December 1994. As bemused aides shook their heads and meditated on how they might deliver on this ambitious pledge, Chiles returned to Tallahassee resolved to do something big, and sooner rather than later.

The unanswered question, of course, was what exactly to do. Administration strategists began bumping into what members of the two task forces of 1989–1991 and the legislative innovators in the House had already encountered: the inexhaustible political blame shifting that parallels and legitimates the economic cost shifting that thwarts health reform. General agreement held that private employers should cover their workers, but mandates were tricky. Business intimated that it could perhaps accept them if honest voluntary efforts failed in the private sector and if insurance costs were properly contained by the public sector. Insurance reform was broadly appealing (even the industry itself endorsed many versions of it), but it was the beginning of workable reform, not the end. Insurers contended, with some merit, that they did not run the larger system and could do little directly to check costs unless hospitals were better disciplined. The hospitals were, as noted above, increasingly receptive to reform, but they insisted as a matter of equity and economics that physicians—those captains of the medical team and dominant allocators of resources—be subjected to the regulation they had so far largely escaped. Physicians, represented by the influential FMA, opposed initiatives that could invite assaults on their incomes and practices. (They were even then sinking heavy political capital into a fight to defeat legislation that would curb widely criticized physician referrals of patients to facilities in which physicians held ownership shares.) If society wants universal coverage, said the doctors, let society make employers offer it.

All of these positions were self-serving, of course, but both logic and politics demanded that they be given their due. Reform would have to be "comprehensive" and "systematic," but these estimable clichés merely underscored the complexity of the problem: What model might improve matters and still win widespread political agreement? In Florida, as elsewhere, consensus on the need for change was well advanced, but each major faction wanted to settle the costs of reform anywhere but on itself. Yet light did glimmer down the tunnel. To be sure, Gordon's single-payer system violated Chiles's preference for a public/private partnership, and Abrams's commission proposal created a new authority too detached from the executive branch (already riddled with cabinet agencies whose heads were chosen by statewide election) to suit the governor. But Chiles's twenty-one-member working group had recommended a new unified health care agency, and the government financing task force had suggested something similar (Fred Jones's 800-pound gorilla). Chiles himself had been promising to get on with a badly needed reorganization of state government. Health care might be just the place to start.

CRAFTING CONSENSUS: BILLS AND BARGAINS

As 1992 arrived, the elements of reform legislation were rapidly falling into place. Although agreement on such deep-reaching substantive departures as mandates and global budgets remained as elusive as before, virtually all public leaders and private groups (except physicians) embraced the notion that a new public-sector entity was surely necessary and perhaps even sufficient to improve the system by 1995. This agreement drew force from many streams of thought that had come to converge under the pressure of costs. A legislative staffer explained: "Consolidation of health functions is an old idea. We here have been working on it for ten years, in fact. But the stars were never aligned right before. Some powerful legislators would want it, but they'd lose office or whatever, and we'd fall short. Various health gurus around Tallahassee wanted it, but they couldn't pull it off." In early 1992 consolidated authority seemed at last to be written in the stars, for reasons summed up by an interest-group participant: "We don't have the answers, but we see we need a process that will help evolution take place." Yet in many ways the consolidated authority remained vague and metaphorical; settling on a structure and bringing it to life in legislation acceptable to House, Senate, governor, and interest groups would require political finesse.

The last stages of consensus crafting and legislative drafting got under way when Rep. Elaine Bloom, a Miami Beach Democrat who chaired the House Health Committee, and her staff began negotiating intensively with other political notables over the details of a bill. On the new authority's general mission most parties concurred. Health policymakers needed a better decision-making structure and process. They should have enhanced capacity to diagnose the workings and failings of the system and to consider the practical implications of change in an integrated context now precluded by organizational fragmentation (Health and Rehabilitative Services was far too diffuse and multifunctional to focus effectively on health or to offer sustained leadership). And they wanted stronger means of concentrating leadership to devise reform plans, work with the governor and legislature to advance them, and explain and define them before the media, the public, and special groups. Most players agreed too that all of the blame- and cost-shifting interests should be given notice that the days of voluntarism and privatism would be numbered if the next round of public, private, and public/private efforts to contain costs and extend access fizzled. Perhaps an explicit "or else" could not be incorporated into legislation (at least not yet), but the bill creating a new authority should leave an "or else" hovering ominously if implicitly in the political air. Broad consensus held that "public/private partnerships" should be the signature of the piece, and this was the truest form of partnership. To those (for instance, the doctors) who groused that "the state was taking over the health system," reformers could rejoin that a better-coordinated public system was the only effective way to get the private system fixed and was (therefore) the only way to save that system.

Against this backdrop, Bloom, a legislator much respected for intellect and negotiating skill, took up the concept of a new public authority and the diverse blueprints for it that important parties entertained and worked to fashion a package that would be acceptable to all. In seeking consent Bloom honored the productive political norm of 1984. As she put it in an interview, "I tried to meet everyone's most important needs." For example, to satisfy business the bill dropped proposed language that would have triggered mandates had the private sector not achieved 95 percent coverage by a certain date. The doctors were sure to object to a reorganization that moved their professional overseers, narrowly focused on credentialing, into a setting that viewed physicians along with everyone else in the big picture of finance and regulation, but some bile might be mitigated by dropping legislative references to fee schedules. Chiles did not want a commission or other administrative species outside the direct line of accountability to his office; the public authority thus would be an executive agency.

The bill produced by Bloom and her colleagues aimed to bring as many as possible of the public institutional fragments addressing health care purchasing and regulation into the newly coherent framework of what came to be called the Agency for Health Care Administration (AHCA). (Florida's constitutional limits on the number of departments in the executive branch blocked that exalted status for the new entity.) All of the animals would be in one tank, as participants were wont to say. The agency would help state policymakers to get the big picture, decide how to fix the system, and then move more directly and forcefully to do it.

The most skillful accommodation could not render the strategy altogether painless. As noted, the FMA would resist a revised regulatory focus; special groups—for instance, the developmentally disabled and the mentally ill—who used Medicaid funds would be less than thrilled to see Medicaid subsumed by a new agency with a focus on financing and regulation; and Florida Health Access, a small-business purchasing cooperative launched in the mid-1980s with Robert Wood Johnson Foundation support and subsidized by state appropriations, would lose a measure of its autonomy. Nonetheless, one protagonist concluded, "The bill was easy to pass because the only giving-up was done by the agencies giving up jurisdiction. No lobbyist or legislators lost anything really." (This verdict may understate the grievances of the FMA, but at this stage it was a less potent political force than one might have expected because it was busy shooting itself in the foot over the "black hat" issue of physician self-referrals.)

The bill sailed unanimously (109–0) through the House, but in 1992 the Senate remained as much a force to be reckoned with as it had been in rejecting the commission bill a year earlier. The FMA carried considerable clout, especially with Senate Republicans, and in any case the Senate had been absorbed mainly in initiatives that emphasized insurance market reform, pooled purchasing, and managed care, not public-sector reorganization. As the Senate began picking the bill apart, supporters of the agency approach grew nervous.

It then grew clear how Bloom's meticulous consensus building might pay off. Supporters of the bill contacted the interest groups they had labored to accommodate and called in their chips. Each group was assigned a senator, whom they lobbied for passage. Aided by strong lobbying from the governor, the bill's proponents performed quick and adroit surgery, grafting the Senate's insurance market reform measures onto the agency initiative and winning Senate passage (35–2) of the amalgamated package, the Health Care Reform Act of 1992.

CONSENSUS FOR WHAT?

By 1990 the states faced growing pressure for health care reform from three powerful sources. First, the uninsured, estimated at about 15 percent of the nonaged U.S. population (about 23 percent in Florida), continued to be a moral embarrassment and an economic burden for institutions beset by cost shifting and uncompensated care. Second, Medicaid spending was raging out of control, increasing at double-digit rates annually and draining scarce resources from other well-defended policy arenas. Third, the nation's continued failure at cost containment had produced an insurance cost crisis that directly hit millions of "uneasily insured" middle-class voters in their (or their employers') pocketbooks. The latter two factors struck with special force in the late 1980s and riveted high-level state political attention on health policy as never before. Politicians heard a chorus of grievances from their constituents and knew they had no choice but to respond.

Although most states confronted these more or less generic forces of political economy, only a half-dozen or so have (to date) marshalled the political will to pass legislation that takes a plausible stab at solutions. As in other unhappy families, each leader state proceeded in its own fashion. Part of the explanation for Florida's activism lies in "objective conditions," especially (1) a politically portentous split between voluntary and public hospitals and their for-profit competitors; (2) decidedly non-Southern support for governmental activism among the state's numerous liberal senior citizens; (3) a governor willing to extend himself farther than most of his peers in promising state reform and in working to advance it; and (4) a nexus of "blue-chip" (senior and savvy) legislators and staffs committed to forcing action and forging compromise.

Even as problems generic to the states cannot explain why a small subset mobilized for action, however, neither can these demographic, economic, and political conditions entirely account for Florida's success in making the political wish the father of the policy deed. To close the explanatory circle, one must give strategic choice due credit. Specifically, a near-decade of state activism spotlights three political gambits that served Florida well. These, as noted above, are the use of commissions and task forces to build awareness and agreement among a wide range of public policymakers and private group representatives; the deployment of policy "clubs" (for example, HB 1) to enhance the relative appeal of more moderate reforms and thereby improve their political prospects; and an emphasis on consensus, on fashioning legislation that tries to honor each group's top priorities and lets each emerge as something of a winner. These strategies effected the practical translation of conditions specific to Florida and of problems common to Florida and other states into the Health Care Access Act of 1984 and the Health Care Reform Act of 1992.

These political dynamics allowed Florida to join the select ranks of leading innovators among the states, but celebration over this undeniable progress should not obscure the limits on what the state found it possible to do in 1992. In early 1993, for example, several smoldering conflicts over structural rearrangements ignited anew. The FMA was (as expected) fighting to rescind the shift of state oversight of physicians from the Department of Professional Regulation to the new agency. Legislators had second thoughts about moving the state employees' health insurance program into the AHCA, its new and presumably proper home. And elements within the Department of Health and Rehabilitative Services and within the special populations it serves continued to wonder whether the Medicaid program would be as sympathetic to their needs in a health care financing and regulatory agency as it had been in a human services setting.

Between the fine intentions proclaimed in the bill and embodied in the AHCA and the achievement of universal coverage and reasonable costs by 1995, moreover, stand many massive obstacles. First, from where and from whom will the money come to secure universal access? New public-sector coverage for the unemployed will demand new public revenues, as presumably will too the subsidies needed to help small business meet the costs of such mandates as may be adopted. Nothing in the law resolves the fiscal dilemmas of a high-growth, small-business, low-tax state. Second, the implications of the AHCA's reform for the wonderful world of private health insurance remain unclear. Health insurance regulation in Florida falls under the purview not of the agency but rather of a separate, cabinet-level insurance commission headed by an elected Republican. A player in the legislative struggles explained: "Insurance is not in the tank because it was politically impossible with an elected Republican insurance commissioner. Ideally you'd want to carve health insurance out, but not all insurance. But it's hard to carve out just health insurance and anyhow it would have mobilized Republican opposition and it wasn't worthwhile to try to do it." An important source of policy fragmentation lives on, with what consequences time will tell.

Third, the state is by no means the sole captain of its fate in steering toward a new system. Its plans will require federal waivers under Medicare, Medicaid, and the Employee Retirement Income Security Act (ERISA).[14] Whether pursued as individual exceptions or as part of new national policies, these will not come easily, yet fundamental reform cannot advance without them. Fourth, the agency may report to the governor, but none of its plans can be adopted without the approval of the legislature, a body subject to continual flux (for instance, Jones has left office and Bloom no longer chairs the House Health Care Committee) and beset by growing partisan rivalry now that Democrats and Republicans have equal representation in the Senate. Fifth, the agency has an enormous and possibly unmanageable agenda. One price of consensus on reorganization is to devolve and defer to the new entity all of the tough questions whose tenacity in eluding legislative resolution made it tempting to buy time by means of reorganization in the first place. A quick scan of the agency's menu of obligations shows (1) securing for each Floridian a "medical home" (a reliable source of primary care); (2) encouraging managed care; (3) pondering reforms in payment systems; (4) proposing a basic benefits list; (5) developing Medicaid buy-ins for the uninsured and a subsidy scheme for hard-pressed small businesses; (6) figuring out what to do about purchaser cooperatives and such; (7) convening research on health outcomes and medical practice parameters; (8) offering recommendations on utilization controls; (9) using the data and recommendations to induce rank-and-file physicians to accept utilization review techniques that control the volume of services; (10) exploring the extension of certificate-of-need (CON) controls to doctors' offices and outpatient facilities; and (11) crafting suggestions for tort reform.

Managing so broad an agenda is a prodigious organizational challenge; not surprisingly, participants and kibitzers differ on how best to proceed. A high-level AHCA official argued, "We've got to look at the big picture. We need fundamental change. It sounds overwhelming, and the key is you can't get killed by details." A hospital representative countered that the big picture is too diffuse and invites fragmentation and dissipation of agency effort. Better, he said, to concentrate on one or two major goals and take on one or two major groups, moving incrementally. Still others recall that the inspiration for the agency is the interconnectedness of health policy problems, which demands both seeing the big picture and doing many big and little things—well and in detail—simultaneously. The public will be watching and expecting great things in 1993 and 1994, proponents contend—the law, after all, pledges that all Floridians will have access to a package of basic health care benefits by the end of 1994—and this will give the agency great clout. But suppose the public does not like what it sees?

Beneath the hardscrabble surface of these tough managerial choices lies political bedrock: Everyone favors universal coverage and cost containment but wants other public or private players to bear the major costs of achieving them. Nothing in the Florida reform reconfigures this political geology. The reform is "merely" the legislative expression of an hypothesis—that reorganization (or, as Alan Maynard would have it, redisorganization) of the public structures and processes that govern health care financing and regulation will enable the state to find the will and the way to major reform. The next two years will presumably test this hypothesis rigorously.

MANAGED COMPETITION IN FLORIDA

In January 1993 testing began in earnest as the AHCA unveiled its preferred general model for reform: the selfsame managed competition that President Bill Clinton also proposed as a national stratagem. On 4 January the agency issued A Blueprint for Health Security, which, among other recommendations, urged that Florida build on such pooled-purchasing prototypes as the Employer Purchasing Alliance, the Florida Healthcare Purchasing Cooperative, and the Florida Health Access Corporation by establishing community health purchasing alliances to concert the market leverage of small groups and individuals. The proposal, said the agency's director, Douglas Cook, was "a market-based partnership which will empower purchasers through the sheer volume of their activities." The premise was that "provider groups, health insurers, and managed care companies must take the initiative to reorganize the health care system at the community level."[15]

After colorful legislative debates, Governor Chiles signed on 29 April the Health Care and Insurance Reform Act of 1993 (consecrated by national coverage on the CBS Evening News). It created eleven Community Health Purchasing Alliances (CHPAs) and imposed significant insurance reforms on the small-group market. The law won wide notice not only because it was the first major product of the reorganization act of March 1992 but also because Florida had become the first state to adopt the reform framework favored by the Clinton administration and has thus made itself a "national model" of sorts.

The Health Care Reform Act of March 1992 put its faith in administrative reorganization. Its progeny, delivered in April 1993, expects big things of economic reorganization in the health insurance market. The newer law, like its predecessor, evokes images of glasses half full and half empty. Florida's version of managed competition is purely voluntary: The CPHAs are available to small businesses, individual purchasers, and the state (acting on behalf of its employees and Medicaid clients) should these buyers find them useful. A legislative staffer observed that progress toward affordable universal coverage requires answers to three questions—how to control costs, how to secure access for everyone, and how to help people who cannot afford coverage—but that the recent legislation directly answers none of them. The 1993 law, like its 1992 antecedent, brought all of the major interests on board (the only significant potential losers are small insurers, whose risk-averting tactics drew near-universal disfavor in Florida, as elsewhere, and arguably physicians, whose prices may face downward pressure) and did so by imposing substantial sacrifices on no one. The law underscores the limits of state health policy innovation: Behind the heroic political crafting and drafting lies the states' inability to decide how broader coverage will be financed and to designate the losses and losers intrinsic to successful cost containment.

On the other hand, managed competition, like the creation of the agency that promoted it, can be viewed as a crucial evolutionary step toward a consensus that probably cannot be constructed for tough measures (for instance, employer mandates or a single-payer system) until less threatening ones have been tried first. It is doubtful whether Florida's voluntary arrangements are a fair test of a theory that (according to Alain Enthoven) requires universal coverage and standard benefits, among other stringent field-leveling rules, in order to stand a chance of working.[16] Moreover, evidence from The Robert Wood Johnson Foundation's Health Care for the Uninsured Program (which helped to launch the Florida Health Access Corporation, among other demonstrations) suggests that voluntary efforts tend to be hobbled by very weak penetration into the small-group market, even for discounted products.[17] But it may not be possible to bypass intermediate measures and go directly to a more "governmentalized" system; one can only hope—at least for now—that federalism plus incrementalism may yet constitute an evolutionary formula for affordable universal coverage.

In the meantime, onlookers understandably disagree about the significance and likely benefits of the legislation of 1992–1993. Some dismiss the measures as pseudo-reform, little more than rearrangements of the deck chairs on the Titanic. One gentle version of this position holds that "this is not a great leap forward but rather Florida positioning itself at the starting blocks for reform." Others contend that the legislation speaks squarely to the realities of health policy today: Consensus on change remains vague, so it has to be focused; the only practical way to do so is to give policymakers and purchasers the institutional tools they need to get to work. The process may be evolutionary, noted one supporter, but both the agency's charge and the implications of managed competition are "pretty radical."

Florida's reforms could turn out to be the boldest or the most timid of the leading innovator states. They could generate macrolevel change on a scale no state has yet dared, or they could end by reflecting and magnifying the many conflicts that impede reform without disclosing reliable means of resolving them. As with the other innovators (save Hawaii), it is as yet impossible to judge whether Florida's dynamics are sound and fury that signify little or nothing or the indispensable structural and procedural preconditions of bold policy change. It would be premature indeed to dismiss the states as leaders in U.S. health policy. It would be equally hasty to pin great expectations on the policymakers now testing new political chemistry in the mysterious laboratory of federalism.

THE BLURRED BIG PICTURE: POLITICAL PATTERNS AND POLICY LESSONS

What, if anything, does the Florida case imply for those who want to understand and accelerate state health policy innovations, or to distill from it lessons for national policy making? An answer must be speculative because the careful comparative work needed to answer the basic question—are Florida and other leading innovators idiosyncratic individual cases, a small set whose members share properties with each other but with few other states, or exemplars of trends that will soon be sweeping the country?—has not been done. In the politically heady summer of 1993 the lure of facile generalization is irresistible, however, so it is argued here that the political patterns that sustained policy advances in Florida are also visible in other reform leaders (notably Hawaii, Massachusetts, Vermont, Minnesota, Washington, and Oregon) and may even offer insights about the requisites of successful reform politics in Washington, D.C.[18]

First, most of the leading reform states prefaced their policy work with numerous and protracted inquiries by commissions and task forces. These bodies performed the same valuable roles as they did in Florida: They educated a wide range of key actors of diverse partisan, ideological, regional, and economic orientations in the complexities of health care reform; created a shared vocabulary and set of foci; and laid personal and intellectual foundations for the legislative process. Along the way, most of these states were accused of substituting talk for action; only in hindsight is it clear how much leisurely conversation promoted confident action in due course. Second, the most vigorous reform states harbor enough "progressive" sentiment to make credible the deployment of policy clubs (especially a single-payer system) should opponents derail more moderate proposals. Vermont, Washington, and the rest are not necessarily "liberal" places, but they, like Florida, had liberal forces of sufficient strength to put and keep "fundamental" reforms on the policy agenda and thereby force a steady search for middle ground. States that have no sentiment for a whole loaf of reform may be unable to concoct half a loaf either. Third, the leading states were all adroit practitioners of the elusive art of legislative-executive relations. All had governors who worked hard to move the reform process along, and all drew strength from the work of astute legislative leaders who mediated differences within and among the ranks of fellow lawmakers, executive branch personnel, and interest-group representatives. The Elaine Bloom role in Florida was played by Nadao Yoshinaga (Hawaii), John Kitzhaber (Oregon), Patricia McGovern (Massachusetts), the "Gang of Seven" (Minnesota), Ralph Wright (Vermont), and Phil Talmadge (Washington), although these were of course leading lights, not solo performers. This is a serendipitous variable that depends on both the supply of legislative/executive skill in high places and the amount of accommodation and cooperation the state's political culture can sustain.

These modest "lessons" may have something to say about national as well as state reform efforts. The contributions of such exploratory bodies as the Pepper Commission and Hillary Rodham Clinton's task force may have less to do with arriving at airtight analytical strategies than with educating important players of diverse values and interests and thus helping to discover ever-broader common ground in the debate about change. The most reliable way to forge consensus on moderate reforms may be to keep alive and well the plausible threat of such "radical" steps as a single-payer system. Certainly the rising sense that such a system might be desirable and feasible as a national reform model helped powerfully to concentrate the minds of myriad interest groups and market advocates on managed competition as an alternative. Without strong presidential commitment, reform may falter, but without the deep support of well-placed legislative leaders who are willing and able to build coalitions that embrace groups as well as legislative peers, executive leadership will stall.

Florida and other creative denizens of the federal system also, however, illustrate the limits of such political lessons for policy outcomes. To date, all of the leading states except Hawaii (and perhaps Washington State) have largely dodged the toughest, truly central questions—how to finance universal coverage and keep it affordable over time. A day of political reckoning will presumably come soon. It is no more—but no less—than a hopeful conjecture that the heroic leaps of strategic faith in Florida and elsewhere will eventually prove to be preludes to affordable universal coverage.

NOTES

1. G.J. Clarke, "Florida's Health Care Access Act: Radical Steps in a Conservative State," *Focus On* (Inter-governmental Health Policy Project, July 1986), 1–22.
2. State of Florida, "Florida Health Care Reform Act of 1992: A Summary" (May 1992).
3. Ibid.
4. Clarke, "Florida's Health Care Access Act," 11.
5. Ibid., 12.
6. Ibid., 15.
7. Ibid.
8. See Florida Task Force on Private-Sector Health Care Responsibility, *Final Report to the Governor and Legislature: Issues and Recommendations* (February 1991); and Florida Task Force on Government-Financed Health Care, *Final Report* (March 1991).
9. Task Force on Government-Financed Health Care, *Final Report*, 5, 6, 8.
10. Ibid., 7.
11. Ibid., 38–39.
12. The quotation is an interviewee's paraphrase of Jones's position.
13. "Summary of House Bill 1: Florida Universal Health Access Plan by Representative Elaine Gordon."
14. The state's waiver agenda is discussed in detail in State of Florida, Executive Office of the Governor, *Federal-State Health Care Issues: Florida's Flexibility Proposal* (April 1992).
15. "Perspectives: Florida Builds on Managed Competition," *Medicine and Health* (18 January 1993).
16. A.C. Enthoven, "The History and Principles of Managed Competition," *Health Affairs* (Supplement 1993): 24–48.

17. W.D. Helms et al., "Mending the Flaws in the Small-Group Market," *Health Affairs* (Summer 1992): 7–27; and C.G. McLaughlin and W.K. Zellers, "Shortcomings of Voluntarism in the Small-Group Market," *Health Affairs* (Summer 1992): 28–40.
18. These reflections on patterns in the federal system owe much to conversations with Michael Sparer of Columbia University.

Hawaii: A Pioneer in Health System Reform

Deane Neubauer

INTRODUCTION

Public officials in Hawaii believe that their state has entered into a "new era of health care." This view is based on a series of recent innovations intended to provide universal access to care and create a health care environment supportive of health promotion and disease prevention. Innovations have focused on meeting challenges within the conventional health care system (consisting primarily of medical care problems) and expanding the boundaries of health care to include matters of broader environmental concern.

Beginning in 1974, with the passage of the Prepaid Health Care Act (Prepaid), the state has moved significantly toward providing universal coverage for its population. More recently, in 1989, with the creation of the State Health Insurance Program of Hawaii (SHIP), Hawaii moved a step closer to providing universal health insurance coverage. In 1990 the state legislature created a Blue Ribbon Panel to investigate the dynamics of the health care system in Hawaii and to propose steps for controlling health care costs. In mid-April 1993, the state announced an ambitious reform of its Medicaid program. Labeled "Hawaii's Health Quest" (Project QUEST), the proposed program is intended to enhance the quality of care while providing universal access, to develop efficient utilization of services while stabilizing costs, and to partially privatize public assistance health care while promoting both effectiveness and efficiency through managed care. Together these initiatives constitute administrators' and legislators' efforts to create Hawaii as "the health state." The current state administration hopes to lead the nation in developing innovative health care proposals while controlling costs—outcomes made possible by an active partnership between public and private sector actors. These have been presented by the state as the "lessons from Hawaii" for American health care reform efforts.

THE SETTING: HAWAII, THE HEALTH STATE

The idea of Hawaii's developing a special character as a health environment began to take form with the election of John Waihee as Governor in November 1986. Many requisite ingredients were already in place. Perhaps most important, Hawaii seems, and is, a healthy place. The fortunes of geography and climate have spared it many of the indignities of industrial and postindustrial development. Its three major industries—tourism, government employment, and agriculture—are clean endeavors when compared with those of smokestack environments. Although there are complex environmental issues that are associated with all three economic endeavors, such as the continued high use of pesticides and herbicides in pineapple and sugar production and infrastructure stress resulting from too rapid tourism growth, these problems are nowhere as great as those associated with traditional industrial development.

Furthermore, the population of Hawaii is on the whole remarkably healthy judged by conventional indicators: with the notable exception of the Polynesians, who in comparison with other groups fare badly on all major health indicators, the longevity of the Caucasians, Japanese, Chinese, Koreans, and Filipinos exceeds that of their mainland counterparts.[1] Hawaii has also become an extremely attractive place to practice medicine. The ratio of physicians to the general population is among the highest in the nation (and indeed the world), although practitioners are highly concentrated in urban Honolulu. Hawaii has slightly more than 4600 physicians and surgeons. Fully 80 percent of these are specialists. Local economic predictions suggest that by the year 2010 health care will be the primary industry in the state, exceeding tourism.

Hawaii's Director of Health, John Lewin, has translated these characteristics of setting, and the health care practices that have grown up within them, into "four lessons" that Hawaii can offer its sister states.

Lesson 1. Primary care works to contain health care costs. Hawaii's health indicators show the following: Hawaii is tied with Vermont in having the lowest infant mortality in the United States; in having the lowest rates of premature mortality in the nation for heart disease (one-third less than national average), cancer (one-fourth less than national average), and lung disease (one-half the national average); in low hospital use (one-third less than national average); and in low emergency room use rates (one-third less than national average).[2]

These outcomes may be explained, Lewin argues, by people's ability to access effective care at reasonable costs and by the fact that Hawaii's doctors historically have emphasized outpatient care. Although Hawaii is a small island state with a highly ethnically diverse population, it is a mistake to think this makes it so unique as to limit comparison. Rather, Lewin argues, what makes health care work in Hawaii is doing standard care correctly: "Early detection of potentially life-threatening conditions results in low premature mortality and low hospitalization. Our people are healthier not because of unique genetics, healthy climate or high-tech medicine, but because they have access to primary care."[3]

Lesson 2. Mandated employer coverage can be an effective tool for universal access. The argument here is that mandated employer coverage levels the playing field for all and yet can be structured to provide significant choice of coverage and payment options (under some circumstances employees can be required to pay portions of the cost). It is notable that in Hawaii most insurance is provided by private nonprofit providers.[4] One fear at the time of Prepaid's passage, namely, that the law would result in a distinctive antibusiness climate and that small businesses in particular would suffer, has not, Lewin contends, materialized.[5]

Lesson 3. Strong insurance reforms must accompany an employer mandate. The key reform is the creation of a community rating, a necessary prerequisite to affordable insurance rates. Hawaii, in part because of the existence of its two nonprofit carriers and the guaranteed market provided by Prepaid, has enjoyed a voluntary rating that has helped to keep rates low.[6]

Lesson 4. Costs can be controlled. Hawaii's health care costs are significantly less than costs in the rest of the United States. Universal access to health care is the key, as the availability of early, inexpensive treatment tends to eliminate later, more expensive care. When all or nearly all persons have access to care, options are then open to insurance companies to pursue strategies that can further control costs. Hawaii also retains its Certificate of Need (CON) process, which has produced a situation in which the state has prevented the creation of excess hospital capacity. This in turn has positively influenced utilization rates. When extended to a significant portion of the population, managed care further reduces costs. Finally, when competition exists within clearly structured ground rules, it forces insurers and providers to hold down costs.

PREPAID HEALTH INSURANCE

In the current national climate, which favors universal coverage, SHIP enables Hawaii to claim that it is ahead of other states in reforming health care. SHIP became a political possibility in Hawaii because of the state's previous experience with the Prepaid Health Care Act of 1974. The law mandates employer-based health care insurance for all employees not covered by collective bargaining. It operates through the existing insurance system, which is dominated by two major providers accounting for 74 percent of existing insurance coverage: the Hawaii Medical Services Association (HMSA—Hawaii's "Blue" organization), which covers 56 percent of all insureds, and Kaiser Permanente (KP), the dominant HMO.[7] The law stipulates that "the plan must provide health care benefits equal to or medically substitutable for benefits provided by plans having the largest number of subscribers in the state." As a result, employees covered under Prepaid would not receive a lesser form of coverage.

The current benefit package includes medical, surgical, and maternity coverage; up to 120 days of hospitalization; outpatient benefits provided by a physician, psychiatrist, or psychologist; diagnostic laboratory services, x-ray, and radiotherapeutic services. Separate insurance statutes create an effect on the "basic benefit package" that Prepaid must offer; in that sense there is a "back door," which amends the effect of the statute with respect to benefit coverage. An impact assessment must be provided by the Legislative Auditor before such authorization. Examples of benefits that have been added to Prepaid coverage through this mechanism include well-baby checkups, mammography, in-vitro fertilization, mental health, and coverage for alcohol and substance abuse treatment.[8]

Financing is shared between employees and employers, with the employee contribution limited to no more than 1.5 percent of total wages; employers must pay at least 50 percent of the remaining cost. Employees are not permitted to refuse coverage, and coverage is universal within the category of nonunionized employees (unions having their own plans.) Certain groups of employees are exempted from coverage, including governmental employees (who have their own plan), approved seasonal agricultural employees, family members in family-owned businesses, certain persons paid on commission, and part-time employees.

Prepaid was the product of plantation culture and a broadly based health agenda sponsored by the state's unions, especially the International Longshore

Workers Union (ILWU). The plantations had provided primary care for their own workers and instilled a sense of employer obligation for health care. As Cora Tellez, vice-president and regional manager of the Kaiser Foundation Health Plan in Hawaii, has put it, "The plantations bred an employer sense of responsibility to care for workers. The state simply became an instrument for expanding that concept to everyone in Hawaii."[9] The pro-labor bias of the law can be seen in the fact that it is administered by the Department of Labor and not by the Department of Health.

The 1974 law was the concluding piece to a 1967 legislative request for studies of temporary disability insurance (which was made law in 1969) and a universal employer-based system of health care. The 1967 act was largely the product of Nadao Yoshinaga, a powerful state senator from Oahu and a primary spokesperson for a Hawaii style of social welfare liberalism. Stefan A. Riesenfeld, a law professor of the University of California at Berkeley, was selected to write both reports. Ironically, part of Riesenfeld's argument for Prepaid lay within the broader political context of the Nixon administration's intentions to develop employer-based mandates on a national level, an outcome that at the time seemed a logical extension to the enactment of Medicare and Medicaid in 1965.[10]

Both Riesenfeld and Prepaid's legislative sponsors targeted coverage for those who were unable to afford medical insurance and yet were unqualified for Medicaid. Estimates of the size of this "gap group" population ran between 11.5 and 17 percent of the population, depending on whether one conflated or kept separate numbers for those under physician and hospital coverage.[11]

Employer-mandated coverage was particularly important to this generation of legislators, who were themselves still close to the plantation experience and who realized that plantation agriculture was on the wane (the number of jobs in sugar and pineapple dropped from some 55,000 in the late 1940s to less than 10,000 by the early 1970s). Ideologically and politically they were also part of the group in Hawaii that led the Democratic Party to majority status in 1954. The legislators were also primarily Japanese-Americans, who had returned from World War II with the dual aims of achieving political power and effecting social justice.

As a vehicle for universal coverage, Prepaid was hamstrung from the beginning, as Riesenfeld had admitted in his report to the legislature. Marvin Hall, current president of HMSA, estimates that subsequent to passage the number of insured workers did not increase by more than 5,000. That is the estimate on the low side. Another observer estimated that at least 46,000 were immediately covered. The differences probably reflect how one counts those who had hospital but not physician coverage and gained both by the act. As Emily Friedman interprets Prepaid's impact, the major effect was not that it provided a massive extension of coverage but "that it defined a basic benefit package, thus setting a standard that all coverage had to meet."[12] Compared with situations within sister states, Hawaii's law has had the effect of constraining the growth of the gap group.

Prepaid was challenged in 1976 by the claim that its authority had been exempted by the Employee Retirement Income Security Act (ERISA) of 1974 (U.S. Supreme Court, Standard Oil v Agsalud, 1976).[13] In 1981, failing to convince the Supreme Court to overturn a lower court ruling, Hawaii saw the Prepaid Act declared void. It was necessary to gain a federal exemption for ERISA to reestablish the law, a result obtained in 1983. Hawaii was the only such state to possess this right throughout the 1980s and early 1990s. While pleased by the success of its congressional delegation in gaining an exemption, the state has nonetheless been bound by its restrictive nature, which prevents further modification without an additional federal authorization.

Although not explicitly intended as cost-controlling legislation, Prepaid's success has in part been put on that outcome. Employer-mandated insurance imposes some measure of rationality on utilization (especially in such areas as early utilization of primary care and emergency room use). Additionally, the program has required very little administrative overhead. Economies achieved by the Department of Labor's relatively parsimonious administration are due in part to the basic duopolistic nature of Hawaii's private insurance industry, which provides coverage for over 85 percent of all insureds. A Premium Supplementation Fund was included in the act to assist small businesses (those with less than eight employees), but over 17 years of the program's administration only a total of $85,000 has been requested. Prepaid is enforced by monetary penalties and by the requirement that the employer is responsible for all the employee's health care costs if coverage is not provided as stipulated.[14]

STATE HEALTH INSURANCE PROGRAM OF HAWAII

The creation of SHIP in 1989 was a self-conscious step to further winnow the gap group while providing comprehensive care and attention to prevention. The latter is, in the opinion of Lewin, the critical element of the three, and the point at which health insurance itself can operate as a lever for social change. He argues that providing health insurance must be conjoined to an active concept of promoting public health, with the first task being to convince people to choose healthy life-styles; the second is to sell health values to business as a solid economic investment; and the third is to move to the broader social agenda of creating a healthy society. As Lewin remarked on the occasion of SHIP's inauguration: "Every health professional and citizen in our state may take pride in the fact that Hawaii is about to make history by implementing the most ambitious health insurance program in the United States."[15]

Like Prepaid, the political strength of SHIP lay in its use of existing provider organizations, thereby being institutionally positioned among market forces that could act to control costs. A major selling point of the program was its presumed ability to affect overall utilization patterns, especially the common tendency of non-insureds to utilize emergency room facilities in lieu of readily available primary care and other more effective screening mechanisms. An attraction to providers was the prospect of reducing the bad debt/uncollectables pool.

The enabling legislation, adopted 28 April 1989, and signed into law in June, provided $4 million for the first 16 months of operation and $10 million for the second full year. State spokespersons have been careful to bill SHIP as "a partnership between government, individuals and families, and the private sector. Government subsidizes insurance coverage for those unable to pay. Insurance companies provide the coverage and the already existing health care providers deliver direct care."[16]

SHIP still does not achieve the goal of providing universal coverage. Rather, it is targeted toward those "who have been uninsured by public or private health care coverage programs and who are at a low enough income level where they cannot access current health care coverage."[17] At the time of SHIP's passage, the size of this group was estimated at 30,000 to 35,000. This number includes a significant number of individuals, often middle-class professionals, who choose to be self-insured for health care. This residual gap group, those in need of coverage, officially estimated at 3.5 percent of the population, is composed primarily of the unemployed (30 percent of the uninsured); dependents of low-income workers, particularly children; part-time workers; off-Oahu residents; immigrants; seasonal workers; and students.

SHIP was but one of two strategies to move closer to universal coverage, the other being an expansion of Medicaid under the options allowed in the various Omnibus "Budget Reconciliation Act" measures passed by Congress in the 1980s and early 1990s. These expansions included pregnant women and infants, young children, elderly persons, and disabled persons. With these additions and the growth in Hawaii/Medicaid's Aid to Families with Dependent Children program, Medicaid grew to cover 96,000 persons by February 1993. Without these expansions those constituting the gap group at which SHIP was directed would have been much larger.[18]

Initially, only Hawaii residents without health insurance coverage in the three months preceding application were eligible for the program. SHIP establishes a sliding fee schedule. Persons whose income is 100 percent below the federal poverty standard pay nothing. Self-payments rise with income. Adults whose income is between 251 and 300 percent of the federal poverty standard pay for the entire cost of insurance, while health care for children is still somewhat subsidized. Only those whose income is below 300 percent of the federal poverty standard are eligible; for Hawaii in 1989, that level was $41,759 for a family of four.[19] To be eligible for SHIP the applicant would need to prove ineligibility for Medicare, Medicaid, CHAMPUS, and Veteran's Administration benefits.[20]

The logic underlying SHIP makes one important assumption and contains another fundamental philosophical premise. First, it is a temporary service, a "hand up" for those in need, "most of whom will be fitting into the Prepaid Health Care system soon"; and second, the emphasis in SHIP will be on preventive and primary care—that is to say, "health" insurance instead of "sickness" insurance.[21] To accomplish the latter, SHIP focuses on services such as health appraisals of which well-baby, well-child care, and age-appropriate health screening would be typical. Also included would be a package of basic primary care items, e.g., 12 physician visits a year with a $5 copayment per visit, laboratory and x-ray, immunizations, etc. (As stated below, these are characteristics of the HMSA version of the program. [See Table 1.]) Larger cost items are deemphasized within the program and where possible shifted over onto Medicaid if spend-downs render the individual Medicaid eligible. Hospitalization is limited to five days, with a dollar limit of $2,500. Two days are allowed for maternity care. Exclusions include elective surgery and high-cost tertiary care. Costly care and procedures such as neonatal intensive care, end-stage renal disease care, and open-heart surgery are shifted where possible onto Medicaid.

Table 1

Summary of SHIP Benefits (HMSA)

PREVENTIVE SERVICES

Well-baby-care Visits
Child physical examinations
Adult physical examinations
Immunizations

OUTPATIENT SERVICES

Physician visits
Diagnostic tests
Radiation and chemotherapy for malignancy
Office, hospital, and ambulatory surgical services

HOSPITAL INPATIENT SERVICES

Room and care
Intensive care
Inpatient ancillary services
Radiation and chemotherapy for malignancy
Physician services
Blood, blood products, and blood bank services

EMERGENCY SERVICES

Emergency room services
Physician services
Automobile ambulance

MATERNITY SERVICES

Physician or nurse-midwife services
Hospital inpatient services
Newborn nursery
Ancillary inpatient services

Source: Hawaii State Department of Health, State Health Insurance Program, HMSA Member Handbook, 1992.

The Department of Health initially estimated that $1.7 million would be obtained from individual payments. In fact, $600,000 was collected from program enrollees. The first-year projection of total coverage was 150,000 enrollee months and a year-end enrollment of 20,000 persons. Contracts for the first year's service were signed by Kaiser (limited to 1,000 Oahu residents) and HMSA.[22] Implementation was designed to identify and enroll people unaccustomed to participation in a medical insurance scheme and/or put off by bureaucratic mechanisms, people who are often viewed as "outside the system." Implementation, which began on 16 April 1990, was statewide and organized to eliminate barriers to entry. Forms were shortened to collect only the most basic information. At present, asset data are not collected. A statewide toll-free number has been made available for those wishing to call for information. Certain persons, such as those dropping off Medicaid rolls, have instant access to the program, as do pregnant women and children. A broadly based community outreach program, assisted by over 200 volunteers trained to help applicants fill out the necessary forms, has also been developed.

EVALUATING SHIP

SHIP's initial evaluation was completed in December 1991. With only a year and a half of real experience, the evaluation study understandably focused more on operational aspects of the program than achievement of its broader goals. It is still not clear whether SHIP can impact a relatively high-risk population with a disease prevention and health promotion strategy that will significantly reduce health care utilization while achieving acceptable health outcomes.

SHIP's initial enrollment goals fell short of expectations, underscoring the difficulties involved in reaching a high-risk population. During the 14-month period (1 June 1990 through 30 July 1991), 12,000 people were enrolled: about 11,000 in the managed fee-for-service plan of HMSA and more than 1,200 in Kaiser Permanente (KP). Disproportionate numbers of enrollees were low-income subscribers: 63 percent from families with incomes below the federal poverty level (FPL) (compared with 10 percent of the state population); 20 percent reported no income at all. With 90 percent of enrollees reporting incomes of less than 200 percent of the Federal poverty level, this population emerges as only slightly better off than Medicaid recipients.[23] By the second year enrollment grew to approximately 17,000 members (some 13,300 in HMSA statewide and 3,500 in KP on Oahu). Together SHIP and an expanded Medicaid program has provided coverage for some 40,000 persons.[24]

One intention of SHIP is to provide a minimal basic benefits package while controlling costs. This initial study does not permit that outcome determination to be made, but utilization rates indicate higher usage in the KP hospital plan, which permits unlimited hospital days. A similar finding holds for ambulatory care. Again, KP allows unlimited visits, while SHIP-HMSA is limited to 12 visits per year for illness care. Utilization by SHIP-KP members is 85 percent higher than utilization by SHIP-HMSA members. The larger proportionate enrollment of poorer families with young children in SHIP-KP may account for these differences.[25]

Interestingly, enrollees prefer SHIP over Medicaid. More than 60 percent of enrollees have incomes less than 100 percent of federal poverty level, rendering some significant portion of this group Medicaid-eligible. Apparently the relative ease of entry into SHIP is a distinct advantage for some, as is the absence of Medicaid's welfare identification. The marketing of SHIP as private insurance is important to many.[26]

The evaluation gives SHIP sound overall marks. It is seen as the result of a set of constructive partnerships in the Hawaii health care environment involving the legislature, affected state departments, providers, and insurance companies. At the time of the initial evaluation, it was clear to many key policy makers that SHIP was inadequate on a number of dimensions. Lewin, for one, saw SHIP as only a stopgap in a still fragmented system, one that does not address the need for increasing funding to public health and community-based prevention programs. Nevertheless, SHIP constitutes Hawaii's central health care program, enabling the state to claim that it is the only one with a workable answer to eliminating the gap group. QUEST would emerge from this sense of incompleteness.

Jim Shon, SHIP's legislative sponsor in the House, has focused on the program's inability to meet what he sees as "the real needs of the community." In his view SHIP gained legislative approval at a time of significant revenue surpluses and at the expense of competing, and ultimately more expensive, programs such as long-term care, which struggled in vain to gain political support from the 1993 legislature. He also believes that the administration of SHIP quickly fell victim to the bureaucratic malaise of the Department of Health, which administers it. It appears that Lewin's enthusiasms for reform have left the Department of Health largely unaffected.

Indications are that applicants increasingly find not the enthusiasm of the early enrollment period, but instead meet a skeptical bureaucracy concerned with controlling "cheating" on self-payment fees. In Shon's view the administration of SHIP chose the narrowest construction of the program to ensure that costs could be controlled, within the $10 million per year figure initially promised the legislature. This trades off against the real potential for SHIP to have provided universal coverage. Shon points to the preamble of the bill he drafted, which called for the legislature to use innovative means to assure coverage for all residents "regardless of age, income, employment status, or any other factor . . . necessary to sustain a healthy life."[27]

Shon and others also question SHIP's actual achievements in coverage. The evaluation report focuses on the continued difficulties of assessing the precise portion of the population without coverage and enrolling these people when found. The report estimates a current gap of 3 to 7 percent, a figure significantly above the official level of 2 percent. In this view Lewin and Waihee, from their intense desire to mark Hawaii as the first state to achieve universal coverage, have canonized SHIP, exporting the myth of universal access. To them these numbers represent "just the last increment" to complete coverage.

Other commentators believe that the uninsured figure may be much higher, noting that the tendency within the state is to estimate the gap group as the residual from total policies in force, a practice that underestimates the percentage of the population with family double coverage. Splitting the difference in estimates, one may be left with the reality of 50,000 uninsureds in the state and the policy embarrassment of having to deal with the cost of uncompensated care which they represent. This sense, too, has quietly supported the movement toward QUEST.[28]

Estimating the portion of the population still not covered by health insurance remains contested terrain. The DOH urges that its estimate of approximately 2 percent has been consistently supported by survey data. The most recent survey, reported in November 1992, finds 3.75 percent without coverage (with confidence limits of 4 percent). From the Department's point of view, these data support its claim that 98 percent of the population enjoys coverage.[29]

THE BLUE RIBBON PANEL

Concern for the lack of integration among the various components and key participants in Hawaii's overall health care environment produced Act 291, Session Laws of Hawaii, 1990, establishing the Governor's Blue Ribbon Panel on Health Care. The Panel was instructed to develop a more comprehensive understanding of the health care system through widespread community consultation, and to develop recommendations facilitative of more effective cost control and application of health care. While acknowledging the key role played by Prepaid and the combination of coverage established by SHIP, Medicaid, the Community Health Nursing Program, and CON, legislators underscored those problems not yet addressed by state legislation, including the burgeoning elderly population, a growing shortage of certain health care professionals, acute-care and long-term-care bed shortages, and dramatically increasing health care costs.

Two important items were excluded from this agenda of concerns: the persistent problems of native Hawaiian health and deficient mental health care programs. The generally poor health of native Hawaiians stands in stark contrast to the generally good health of the rest of the population. The reasons for this poor health profile are numerous and subject to considerable and contentious differences of emphasis and interpretation. Where many see the issue as one of improving access to medical care for Hawaiians, others, including many activists within the native Hawaiian community, see the issue in the broader perspective of cultural conflict between Hawaiian and "modern" lifestyles. These issues have been addressed in part through the Native Hawaiian Health Care Act passed by Congress in 1988. The law is currently in the early stages of implementation, and it is too early to assess its likely impact on the overall health of Hawaiians.[30]

Introducing the Blue Ribbon Panel on 7 December 1990, the governor stressed that the Panel "represents a cross-section of Hawaii's economic and social leaders including representatives of business, insurance providers, unions, academia, consumers, government agencies and health care providers."[31] The actual appointment of the 23 members proved an act of delicate political maneuvering for the Governor's office, which struggled to balance the reality of existing vested interests with the prospect that the Panel might actually break new ground.

The Panel met almost biweekly for more than 15 months. In July 1992 it reported out 36 recommendations directed at controlling costs in five areas: administrative costs; medical malpractice; consumer expectations; health care resources; and cost shifting. These five areas, chosen after months of hearing the views of a wide sector of the health care community, are significant in part for what they did not include. Long-term care, certainly a major factor in the overall cost environment, was not addressed because the Governor's Office on Aging was concurrently preparing its own recommendations. The Panel's authorizing legislation identified some specific areas for attention, including insurance rate regulation, health care facility costs, and common purchasing agreements, as areas for panel attention. The first two were rejected after considerable discussion because they were seen more as the result than the cause of costs. Joint purchase was seen as already a routine administrative practice. In extending the Panel's original one-year authorization, the legislature suggested that mental health issues were also a matter of concern, but the final report makes no mention of mental health issues.

The Panel designated 8 of its 36 recommendations as "key change" proposals, so designated because of their presumed centrality to the overall pattern of reform being advocated by the Panel. These proposals were as follows:

1. Reform of administrative procedures, including electronic claims processing, automated record keeping, and a universal claims form.
2. Reform of the regulatory system to lessen the costs of regulatory compliance.
3. Reform of insurance access by developing a revised community rating.
4. Development of a no-fault medical malpractice system.
5. The addressing of shortages in health care human services, primarily through better strategic planning.
6. Efforts to modify consumer expectations for the health care system through more efficient and effective utilization practices, the establishment of a universal basic benefit package, and more effective use of primary care as first access to the system.
7. Eliminating cost shifting by fully funding public support programs, which cover all public benefit packages.[32]

The eighth key change recommendation grew out of the panel's concern that its work result in actual changes in the current system. It called for the creation of an "entity" to implement the panel's recommendations. This broad, sweeping recommendation extended beyond the Panel's legislative mandate. The consortium called for in the recommendation explicitly combined private and public sector players in an extensive range of activities, including the gathering, analysis, and dissemination of system-wide data (to make better judgments about cost issues); the implementation of Panel recommendations; the redesignation and monitoring of the basic benefits package; and periodic legislative recommendations on other health care matters.

The Panel believed this to be its most important recommendation and spent the most time on its deliberation. For some of the key players the creation of this entity could only arise from previously cordial working relations between the key public and private sector players, particularly the insurance industry. (in other words, the coalition that produced both Prepaid and SHIP). On this score the entity signaled a further commitment to "partnership" in the development of quasi-cooperative, quasi-regulatory approaches to further health care system development and cost control. Others on the panel were less sanguine, calling the entity's nature neither "fish nor fowl" and predicting that it would either be ineffective or dominated by the insurance/provider industry. Business interests on the panel predictably were reluctant to embrace what they called "yet another" increment of public sector regulation. Those representing labor interests argued that without substantial governmental authority and backing such an entity would not be taken seriously.

The goal of the Panel was to see its findings translated into administrative recommendations for legislative action. The two most important provisions were those calling for a community rating for health care and for the creation of "the entity." Each was proposed as legislation by the Department of Health, and both failed to gain legislative support. A "face-saving" Senate resolution was gained on the community rating issue; it requested the Legislative Reference Bureau to study the feasibility of requiring community rating of all small-group health service plans providing coverage in Hawaii. Some administrative supporters hope that this mechanism will prove a vehicle for developing the data-gathering, policy-analysis elements of the proposed entity, thereby keeping them abreast of other states that have recently brought health care commissions into being.

Part of the defeat of these bills can be ascribed to an error in tactics committed by the administration, which after the initial presentation of a bill to create a Health Care Commission modified that submission under pressure from the Department of Health. Consequently, the newly created commission within the existing health planning organization (the State Health Planning and Development Agency [SHDPA]) was shut down. The SHDPA obviously was concerned that the data-gathering and analysis functions, envisioned by the Blue Ribbon Panel's entity and assigned to the original commission, would undercut its existing writ.

The Department of Health, of which SHDPA is an administrative part, sought to mollify SHDPA by tying it to the new commission, hoping in the process to leave undisturbed the CON activities of the agency (Lewin is convinced the CON activities contribute significantly to Hawaii's efforts to control the creation of surplus capacity).[33] Perhaps unexpectedly, this intradepartmental political compromise ran directly against the view of most Blue Ribbon Panel members, whom Lewin had hoped would strongly support his commission proposal. Their notion of an entity was something that had been positioned away from conventional regulatory turf. Lacking a broad base of support, this concept of a commission quickly broke down. When it was followed by an even weaker version than the original, creating in effect a shell commission useful mainly for pursuing external grants directed at issues of cost control and data collection, the bill satisfied virtually no one and was easily defeated.

What occurred was a breakdown in the political coalition that supported both SHIP and Blue Ribbon. Jim Shon lost his committee chairmanship to a wide-sweeping reorganization of the House just before the 1993 legislative session. The new committee chair, Representative Julie Duldulao, proved either unwilling or unable to forge a new coalition to support health reform matters. Lewin, increasingly out of state and involved with the Clinton Health Care Task force, found the leadership ties he had used to bring others on board in support of administrative proposals dwindling with his increased absence. Some observers of the process, Jim Shon foremost among them, have been pointed in their criticism of the state's loss of relative position vis-à-vis other states on health care reform. Lewin himself regards the 1993 legislative session as a disappointment. "It wasn't a progressive session," he remarked at the session's close, "but I look forward to less conservative times."[34]

PROJECT QUEST

Throughout the health care reform process of the past three years, costs have continued to increase for private insurers and government. Both HMSA and Kaiser have increased insurance rates by 14 to 18 percent over the past several years, and these increases belie the generally favorable experience Hawaii has had in limiting costs. (Part of Hawaii's claim to distinction is that it spends only 7.8 percent of the state product on health care, whereas an expenditure of 13 to 14 percent is characteristic of the nation as a whole.) Medicaid expenditures have also continued to rise in part as a response to continued program expansions. This year the state legislature was forced to appropriate an additional $35.3 million to continue Medicaid funding through June; additionally, state government imposed a 4 percent provider tax on both hospitals and nursing homes. QUEST has developed an insurance purchasing pool for both Medicaid and SHIP, folding most recipients under a single insurance coverage plan.[35] The state hopes to contain its costs through the promotion of managed competition for all publicly funded patient coverage, through the development of a comprehensive purchasing cooperative to be located with the

Department of Human Services, and by the creation of a basic benefit plan common to both Medicaid and SHIP recipients.

As Prepaid anticipated the health reforms of the Nixon administration, so has QUEST anticipated managed competition as a major feature of the Clinton health care initiatives, hoping to develop it in Hawaii first. The broad assumption that underlies this strategy is that the current ERISA exemption will be extended and modified to permit these changes. Current proposals modifying the exemption and Prepaid to complement the changes in QUEST include providing dependent coverage, changing the employer/employee share ratio (without hurting lower-income employees), and of course changing aspects of the benefit package. Throughout the discussion of national health care reform during the past two years, Hawaii's political leaders have been concerned that the state not lose whatever leverage it has gained over time by being forced to conform to national proposals that would reduce coverage in any way. In this sense QUEST can be seen as both preemptive and as an extension of the rationale to pursue universal coverage while controlling costs and continuing to provide a desirable basic benefit package.

The key to cost control within QUEST is the substitution of conventional insurance coverage for the open-ended payment scheme of Medicaid, utilizing conventional, if modest, copayments for the most major kinds of coverage. Although early versions of the program suggested that the overall "richness" of Medicaid would be reduced through QUEST, more recent versions including the recently formulated RFP states that the health plan "shall provide, at a minimum," whatever services are currently required by Medicaid. This is a disappointment for conservative health care professionals and business representatives, who have seen the existing Medicaid package as excessively generous. The primary care and prevention emphases of SHIP have been carried over into QUEST.

QUEST provides adult medical services including inpatient hospital services for medical, surgical, rehabilitative, and maternity/newborn care; outpatient hospital care; preventive services; prescribed drugs including blood and blood products; radiology, laboratory, and other diagnostic services; physician services; maternity services; other practitioners; therapeutic services; durable medical equipment; corrective appliances and artificial aids; and home health services and hospice services. Children's medical services are defined as EPSDT (Early and Periodic Screening, Diagnosis and Treatment) services, a federally mandated program emphasizing prevention and early detection of medical, dental, and behavioral health conditions and timely treatment. Adult and children dental services are to be provided, as will catastrophic care on a shared responsibility basis (over $30,000 the state bears the financial burden). Both adult and child behavioral health services are provided for mental health, drug abuse, and alcohol abuse.[36]

Representatives of the provider industry, hospitals in particular, are enthusiastic about QUEST because they see it as ending cost-shifting, a major goal of the Blue Ribbon process. "That," in the view of Richard Meiers, president and chief executive officer of the Healthcare Association of Hawaii, "[is] what really sends the cost of health care up in Hawaii every year." Meiers holds that Hawaii's hospitals were shortchanged $38.8 million in 1992. Small business owners look for the program to relieve HMSA and Kaiser of the necessity to raise rates drastically to spread the shortfall over other subscribers.[37]

To date only some physicians have been vocal in their opposition to QUEST, seeing in it an extension to managed care, which prevents individuals from choosing their own physicians. Dr. Philip Hellreich, the legislative chair of the Hawaii Federation of Physicians and Dentists, the state's most politically conservative health professional interest group, has gone so far as to predict that if managed care programs become the norm, many of Hawaii's "finest physicians will leave the state." But this is a decidedly minority view, representative of attitudes that Robert Alford has termed those of "a sovereign profession."[38] The current president of the Hawaii Medical Association, Jeanette Chang, is more prosaic: "We need some kind of reform, because Medicaid has gone down the tubes."[39] Welfare advocates have objected throughout the formulation process that QUEST threatens to reduce existing benefits enjoyed under Medicaid. The expanded coverage represented in RFP suggests that this view has come to be shared by state administrators who have now opted for a "richer" overall package of benefits. Jim Shon continues to caution that QUEST will continue to individualize solutions for broadly based medical and health problems at the expense of community-based programs such as Honolulu's community health clinics.

CONCLUSION

Hawaii's health reform efforts are lodged somewhere in midstream. Just how large that stream might be and the nature of the direction are under dispute. Until two years ago Hawaii unquestionably led the nation in developing near universal coverage while keeping health care costs under control. The health care environment in the state was remarkable for the amount of cooperation existing between the private and public sectors and the seemingly broad consensus existing on the major dimensions of health care reform. The outcomes of the Blue Ribbon Panel signaled the possibility of yet another step forward toward this productive partnership, and as we have seen, the state's leaders continue to emphasize Hawaiii's leadership in many areas of health care provision and financing.

Health care professionals and lay policy-watchers are uncertain about what lies in the near future for Hawaii. Some of this uncertainty reflects concern over the Clinton health care proposals and their potential effect on Hawaii. For local reformers such as Lewin, Project QUEST is a step closer to his goal of providing a "seamless" system of health insurance and care, coupled with an emphasis on health promotion and disease prevention. Pushing QUEST to conclusion in alliance with the Department of Human Services is a major policy success for the reformers, especially since so much of it has taken place in the administrative rather than the legislative arena. The concern of Lewin and others promoting QUEST is to make sure that no part of a national health care program would reduce or contract the gains that they have already achieved in Hawaii.

Yet for others, some element of purpose and vision seems to have been lost over the past year of health reform efforts. Certainly the legislative session failed to contribute anything substantial to a broad-based reform program, and in comparative terms during the same period several states have moved beyond Hawaii through the development of health care commissions. These are becoming vehicles for informing public policy through the systematic gathering of public data on a range of health care questions, including those of enforced community ratings. Those inclined to be pessimistic see the failures of 1993 as symptomatic of a decline in a broadly based political will to continue health care reform. As one business leader remarked in the follow-up to the Blue Ribbon Process, "People are just not convinced that a problem exists [that is] important enough for us to go beyond tinkering with what we already have."

A more optimistic view puts the whole of the 1993 legislative session in broader context. One dimension is basic structural change occurring with Hawaii politics, change deriving from the same set of forces that cost Jim Shon his committee chairmanship in the House. Realignments are taking place within the dominant Democratic Party, which has run Hawaii politics for the past three decades. The play between Oahu and neighbor island delegations is becoming more intense. Other lines of cleavage within the legislature are also emerging as new members seek leadership positions. Moreover, the 1994 elections will produce a new governor. The legislature acts as if it is already beginning to anticipate that event, and one result is a lack of coherence in the legislative agenda.

Another explanation invites consideration of more prosaic factors, most especially the effects of Hurricane Iniki in September 1992. In times of such widespread devastation, Hawaii is reminded both of its relatively small size in the world and its significant vulnerabilities. The legislature and administration spent an enormous amount of energy dealing with the aftermath of the hurricane, an event made worse by the budgetary turndowns that had immediately preceded it. In this view, the legislature was in no mood for another bout of adventuresome health care reform. There is also the general question, What stands for success in health care reform anyway?

Skilled administrative players point out that the normal sequence of events for reform legislation is that several legislatures are required for a major reform to gain the familiarity necessary to build a successful coalition about it. This was certainly true for both workers' compensation and Prepaid. Part of what makes this session seem so much like a failure, this argument suggests, is the atypical success of SHIP, which sailed through one legislative session and was ready for implementation within months. These players believe that continued reforms are far from dead and will be resurrected in the next legislative session.

In the meantime QUEST will bear the banner of reform in Hawaii, one that continues to advance the claim that only this state significantly approaches the goal of providing its citizens with universal health care coverage. Until that can be said of some national program, or of states that move in advance of a national program, Hawaii will continue to stand alone on this dimension of health care reform.

ACKNOWLEDGMENTS

Robert Grossman, John Lewin, James Shon and Peter Sybinsky read an earlier draft of this paper, providing valuable information and insights. Bill Dendell has been very helpful in providing data. I want to thank them for their contributions.

NOTES

1. John Lewin and Peter Sybinsky report on two recent national analyses of the comparative health of the 50 states, one by Northwest Life Insurance Company (Milwaukee) and the other by the American Public Health Association, which rate Hawaii first among the states on their indicators. John C. Lewin and Peter A. Sybinsky, "Hawaii's Employer Mandate and Its Contribution to Universal Access," *Journal of the American Medical Association*, 269(1993): 2538–43.

   The overall death rate of Native Hawaiians is 34 percent higher than that for the total United States population. Eldon Wegner, "A Framework for Assessing Health Needs," *Social Process in Hawaii*, 32(1989). In addition Hawaiians have a 50 percent higher infant mortality rate and a 61 percent higher chronic liver disease in comparison with the rest of the state. The incidence of diabetes is 222 percent and heart disease 44 percent higher than the national average (Source: Statistics presented by Office of Hawaiian Affairs to Board of Health 1992).
2. The following is taken directly from a document Lewin has developed to provide a thumbnail sketch of Hawaii's health care system, a campaign document, as it were. John C. Lewin, MD., "Briefing on Hawaii's Health Care System," (ND), Hawaii State Department of Health.
3. Lewin, "Briefing," p. 8.
4. An additional advantage has been HMSA's historic record of controlled administrative costs. HMSA argues that 94 cents of every client dollar goes to care reimbursement, which certainly compares very favorably with other mainland Blues and may in fact be the lowest administrative overhead cost factor in the United States.

5. See also Lewin and Sybinsky, "Hawaii's Employer Mandate." This assertion is hotly contested by small business and its lobbying agents, who see Lewin's effort to reform Prepaid (so that all employers, no matter how small, would be affected) as harming them. The news reports the day after Lewin presented Seamless to the Blue Ribbon Panel chose to emphasize his proposal for extending Prepaid to include part-time employees, most of whom work for small businesses. The outcry was considerable and overshadowed any other positive press that Seamless might have received from the broader community.
6. The Blue Ribbon Panel had a difficult time settling on a recommendation covering the community rating. In Hawaii it has become a little bit of all things to all people. Kaiser and HMSA argue for the concept of the voluntary rating, which Lewin promotes for the purposes noted. Others, however, believe that a significant erosion has occurred in the concept because it works significantly to the disadvantage of small businesses, which are in effect small-risk pools. The rating has nine "bands" that can be assigned to applicants, with fully 45 percent difference between the most and least favorable. In the eyes of many this undermines the effect that a community rating is meant to produce, namely, fully homogenizing the risk pool.
7. In 1990 HMSA enrolled 605,127 persons; Kaiser, 179,450; and Island Care, a more recently developed HMO, 22,337. *The State of Hawaii Data Book: A Statistical Abstract*, Department of Business, Economic Development and Tourism, 1990, p. 384.
8. Lewin, "Briefing," p. 4.
9. Quoted in Emily Friedman, *The Aloha Way: Health Care Structure and Finance in Hawaii* (Honolulu: Hawaii Medical Service Association Foundation, 1993), p. 57.

10. Stefan A. Riesenfeld, *Prepaid Health Care in Hawaii*, University of Hawaii, Legislative Reference Bureau, Report No. 2, 1971. Note Riesenfeld's reasoning (p. 9): "The newest development in the field of compulsory health insurance is the President's announcement of his Family Health Insurance Plan for children. . . . Legislative proposals are promised for January 1971. . . . Finally, it should be noted that the general desirability of prepayment plan protection against medical cost was again strongly stressed in the June 1970, Recommendations of the United States Department of Health, Education and Welfare, Task Force on Medicaid and Related Programs."
11. State of Hawaii, *House Reports*, 1974.
12. Friedman, *The Aloha Way*, p. 64.
13. Standard Oil of California objected to the legislature's mandate to include alcohol and drug treatment within the basic benefit package.
14. Lewin and Sybinsky, "Hawaii's Employer Mandate," p. 2538.
15. John Lewin, "From Vision to Reality: Insurance Plan Establishes Hawaii as the Health State," *Hawaii Health Messenger* (State Department of Health), 52, No. 2(1989), p. 1.
16. John Lewin, "Hawaii's System of Universal Access to Health Care Coverage," address to the Advisory Council on Social Security, Department of Health and Human Services, 27 July 1990. p. 3.
17. Lewin, "Hawaii's System," p. 3.
18. Lewin and Sybinsky, "Hawaii's Employer Mandates," p. 2540.
19. There is no discernible compelling logic for this figure. Apparently Lewin and his Health Department colleagues felt that level would both sell politically and was a realistic assessment of living costs in Hawaii, which typically has the highest cost of living in the nation.

20. Lewin, "From Vision to Reality," p. 1.
21. State Department of Health document, 21 April 1990.
22. Because Kaiser offers a package with far more benefits than HMSA, it has continued to restrict enrollment in the program as a protection against excessive exposure.
23. "*The State Health Insurance Program of Hawaii: From Legislative Priority to Reality*," prepared by Center for Health Research, Kaiser Permanente, Portland, Oregon; School of Public Health, University of Hawaii at Manoa, Honolulu, Hawaii; and Hawaii Medical Service Association Foundation, Honolulu, Hawaii. 10 December 1991, p. 7.
24. Lewin and Sybinsky, "Hawaii's Employer Mandate," p. 2540.
25. "*The State Health Insurance Program of Hawaii*," p. 8.
26. *The State Health Insurance Program of Hawaii*," p. 19.
27. Hawaii State Legislature, 1989, HB No. 1906, p. 2.
28. Gerard Russo, health economist at the University of Hawaii, is one person making this argument. Russo worked as a technical consultant to the Blue Ribbon Panel.
29. Hawaii Department of Health, "Measuring the Uninsured Population in Hawaii," 6 November 1992, pp. 1–21.
30. For a recounting of the process leading to the passage of the Native Hawaiian Health Care Act and a statement of the broader cultural argument, see Kekuni Blaisdell, "Historical and Cultural Aspects of Native Hawaiian Health," *Social Process In Hawaii*, 23(1989).
31. News release from the Executive Chambers of the Governor, 7 December 1990, p. 1.
32. *Report of the Governor's Blue Ribbon Panel on Health Care*, September 1992.

33. Lewin and Sybinsky, "Hawaii's Employer Mandate," p. 2539.

34. Linda Hosek, "Health Bills Didn't Get Intensive Care, Medical Pros Say," *Honolulu Star Bulletin*, 4 May 1993, p. a-1B.

35. The plan would exclude approximately 25,000 aged and disabled persons who would continue to be served by Medicaid in a traditional manner. The rationale is that these persons have needs that stand outside the requirements of the basic benefit package. Helen Altonn, "State Overhauls Health Care Plan," *Honolulu Star Bulletin*, 15 April 1993, pp. 1, A-8.

36. Hawaii Health QUEST: Request for Proposal for QUEST Health Plan, State of Hawaii, Department of Human Services, September 1993, 108 pages.

37. *Honolulu Star Bulletin*, 15 April 1993.

38. Robert Alford, *Health Care Politics* (Chicago: University of Chicago Press, 1976).

39. Kevin Dayton, "Concerns Voiced on Health QUEST Plan,"*Honolulu Advertiser*, 26 April 1993, pp. A-3, a-12.

Minnesota: The Trip From Acrimony to Accommodation

Howard M. Leichter

INTRODUCTION

In the fall of 1991 Minnesota politics was a microcosm of national politics: the state was running a huge budget deficit, it had a Republican governor who was suffering the highest disapproval rate (55 percent) of any Minnesota governor in nearly a half century, the Democrats controlled both houses of the legislature (as they had done in all but four years since 1973), but without a veto-proof majority, and public opinion polls indicated that a majority of Minnesotans were concerned about health care and health insurance costs. Even so, on 3 June 1991, Governor Arne Carlson (IR)[1] vetoed the Health Care Access Bill, which would have completely revamped the state's health insurance system and moved Minnesota toward universal access to health care. Carlson's veto bucked strong public support for reform, and although the governor did not face reelection in 1992, the entire state legislature did. Citizens were expressing dissatisfaction with state government, and an unprecedented number of legislators were contemplating retirement.

Ten months later, Governor Carlson and the Gang of Seven (a group of four Democrats and three Republicans responsible for the health care reforms) stood arm in arm with the state's House and Senate leadership in the governor's reception room and announced to the press that they had reached agreement on a bipartisan plan to reform the state's health care system. The bill (House File [HF] 2800), originally called HealthRight, promised to contain health care costs, expand access, reform health insurance, and put Minnesota at the very forefront of health care reform in the nation.[2] How and why the state's political leadership moved from acrimony to accommodation provides a fascinating glimpse into the changing character of health care politics in America. Also, the story of the compromise may offer a possible model for accomplishing reform in the states and national government.

Among the lessons the Minnesota experience offers are the following: first, rapprochement between Republicans and Democrats occurred when each realized that cost containment and expanding access were intrinsically related. As Minnesota's senate minority leader Duane Benson (IR) put it: "The first thing we have to do is bring down the cost and use the savings to increase accessibility."[3] Second, political leaders in Minnesota recognized that health care reform was now a middle-class issue that could be ignored only at great peril to one's political future. This bit of political wisdom was new to Republicans, who traditionally have not viewed health reform as one of "their issues." Third, there is a need to rewrite the conventional wisdom on interest group politics, especially with regard to the role of health care providers. Health care reform in Minnesota advanced despite fierce opposition from the state's powerful medical lobby.

HEALTHRIGHT: PROVISIONS OF THE LAW

The Minnesota law reflects an emerging national health reform agenda: contain costs, expand access, reform health insurance, deal with the peculiar problems of health care in rural areas, collect health care data, and find some way to finance expanded access (see Table 1).

At the heart of the law is cost containment. Indeed, it is a measure of the times in general, and the political dynamics of Minnesota in particular, that Article I deals with cost containment, while the issue of access is taken up 60 pages and three articles later in the legislation. Minnesota, like every other state in the nation, has recently experienced a rapid escalation in health care costs. Total government spending on medical assistance increased 41.4 percent from 1985 to 1990 (from $992.7 million to $1.403 billion). The private sector, too, experienced this problem. In 1991 Minnesota ranked 9th in the nation in terms of average health payments per family; the average family expenditure was $7,252, up from $2,936 in 1980. In 1991 the Minnesota Health Care Access Commission found that "*The current health care system is unaffordable for many Minnesotans* [emphasis added]. One in three uninsured Minnesotans have unpaid medical bills, averaging $826. One in five individually insured Minnesotans have unpaid medical bills, averaging $1,207."[4]

It is not surprising, then, that the legislative finding introducing Article 1 described the "devastating effect on the health and cost of living of Minnesota" due to the "staggering growth in health care costs." It went on, however, to link cost control as "essential to the maintenance of the many factors contributing to the quality of life in Minnesota: our environment, education system, safe communities, affordable housing, provision of food, economic vitality, purchasing power, and stable population."[5] As Table 1 indicates, HealthRight takes a largely regulatory approach to controlling health care costs. It establishes a Health Care Cost Containment Commission that, along with the state's health care commissioner, will attempt to control costs by doing the following:

1. Setting a target for slowing health cost inflation by 10 percent per year beginning in 1993;
2. Establishing statewide and regional limits on total spending;
3. Fostering regional health care planning;
4. Imposing constraints on health care providers by monitoring, retrospectively, capital expenditures on expensive (in excess of $500,000) technology;
5. Reviewing the effectiveness and outcomes of various treatment methods (i.e., so-called practice parameters); and
6. Encouraging individual health promotion efforts through health education and wellness programs.

TABLE 1

Major Provisions of HealthRight Cost Containment

- Creation of a 25-member state health care commission that will set an "annual limit on private and public spending on health care services for Minnesota residents." The commission will submit a plan to the legislature for slowing the rate of growth by at least 10 percent per year beginning in July 1993.
- The commissioner of health will "establish statewide and regional limits in total health care spending."
- Creation of six regions in the state to foster regional planning and coordination of health care delivery in order to help monitor and manage cost controls.
- The commission will monitor and promote practice parameters among health care providers.
- The commissioner will designate "centers of excellence" for specialized and high-cost procedures and treatments and establish minimum standards and requirements for these.
- Encourage, through education and wellness programs, health promotion through greater individual responsibility in health care.
- Define and place restrictions on conflicts of interest where providers profit from making professional referrals.
- Phase out, over three years beginning 1 January 1993, balance billing of Medicare patients.
- After 1 April 1992, the commissioner of health will retrospectively report major technology purchases in excess of $500,000 to determine their necessity.

Health Insurance Reform

- Restricts factors used by health insurance companies to determine premiums (i.e., underwriting): gender-based rating is prohibited; sets limits on variation above or below average rates (bands) based on health status, occupation, geographic location, and age.
- Prohibits insurers from denying coverage to small businesses, or from refusing to renew individual or group policies.
- Creates two new, low-cost insurance plans that insurers must offer to small businesses.
- Sets minimum-loss ratios in both the small group (75 percent, increasing to 80 percent) and individual (65 percent, increasing to 70 percent) markets.
- Allows private businesses to join a state-sponsored insurance purchasing pool.
- The commissioner of commerce shall recommend to the legislature, by 1 February 1993, standardized health care insurance forms.

Expanding Access to the Uninsured (HealthRight)

- Eligibility: Beginning October 1992, family members of children enrolled in the state's Children's Health Plan (for children in families with incomes of 185 percent of the federal poverty level) will be eligible for subsidized health insurance. Premiums will be based on a sliding scale depending on income and will range from 1.5 percent of monthly income for the lowest income earners to 8 percent for the highest. The program will be expanded in January 1993 to families with children who have incomes of up to 275 percent of the poverty level, and in January 1994 to all uninsured Minnesotans who have not had health insurance coverage for four months, not had access to employer-subsidized insurance for 18 months, and who are Minnesota residents and have lived in the state for at least six months.

- Coverage: Initially HealthRight will cover only primary and preventive care. Beginning in July 1993, it will add inpatient hospital care up to $10,000, with a 10 percent copayment for adults, and an out-of-pocket maximum of $2,000 per individual and $3,000 per family. There will also be copayments for prescription drugs, eyeglasses, and nonpreventive dental care.

Financing

- Cigarette Tax: Beginning 1 July 1992, the state cigarette tax will increase by 5 cents per package. Revenue from this increase will be used to provide start up funds for the program. (After two years the revenue will go into the General Fund.)
- Hospital Tax: Beginning 1 July 1993, a 2 percent tax will be levied on hospital gross patient revenues. This tax may be passed on to third-party payers during the first year only.
- Health Care Provider Tax: Beginning 1 July 1994, a 2 percent gross revenues tax will be levied on health care providers. The tax may not be passed on to third-party payers.
- Nonprofit Health Service Plans: Beginning 1 July 1996, a 1 percent gross premium tax on nonprofit health insurers (e.g., Blue Cross/Blue Shield, HMOs).

Rural Health Care

- Creation of a 15-member Rural Health Advisory Council to advise the commissioner of health on rural health issues, and creation of an Office of Rural Health to implement rural health initiatives, including providing funds to help financially troubled hospitals switch to other economic endeavors.
- State will provide financial assistance to financially troubled rural hospitals.
- The state will implement a loan forgiveness program for physicians practicing in rural areas.

- The University of Minnesota will take steps to increase the number of primary care graduates and reduce the number of specialists.

Data Collection and Research Initiatives

- Creation of a Health Care Analysis Unit to collect and analyze data on health care costs and existing practice parameters (i.e., the effectiveness and outcomes of different treatments), and to develop and recommend new parameters.

The Minnesota plan also will offer subsidized health insurance policies to the estimated 370,000 Minnesotans who are uninsured for all or part of the year. This figure represents about 7 percent of the state's population, although it is well below the national average of nearly 14 percent. Nevertheless, as the Health Care Access Commission noted, about 11,000 Minnesotans were refused health care in 1990, and an additional 50,000 were delayed in seeking care for serious or moderately serious conditions.[6] This part of the plan builds on the highly successful Children's Health Plan (CHP). Established in 1988, CHP provides health care to children in families with incomes of 185 percent (and below) the federal poverty level. HealthRight, initially, will extend coverage to the families of these children. In 1993 it will apply to families with children whose incomes fall below 275 percent of poverty; and in 1994, to all Minnesotans who have been uninsured for at least four months and have not had access to employer-based insurance for 18 months. By July 1993 coverage will include both inpatient and outpatient care, but with a $10,000 maximum on inpatient care and with various copayments. Finally, it is important to note here that despite the inflated rhetoric that accompanied passage of the law, HealthRight will not bring about universal access to health care in Minnesota.

Under the most optimistic of estimates, by 1997 the law will provide health coverage to only about 40 percent of uninsured Minnesotans. It will not ensure universal coverage because there are no individual or employer mandates, and it carries insurance copayments for many who will choose not to participate.

HealthRight also addresses the cost and accessibility of private health insurance for the non-poor. The Health Care Access Commission had found that 366,000 Minnesotans (8.5 percent of the population) "have individual insurance marred by high premium costs, high deductibles and stringent insurance underwriting policies which can result in policy denials, cancellations or pre-existing condition exclusions."[7] Although many reformers favored community rating for individual and small group markets, so strong was Republican opposition to this idea that there was little discussion of it. Hence, the law only went as far as eliminating gender-based rating and setting up limits on different rates that insurers can charge for occupational and health status. The law, however, does prohibit insurers from denying coverage to small employers because of the risks involved in their business or the health status of their employees. Finally, the law makes the purchase of health insurance more affordable to businesses by allowing them to join a state-sponsored insurance pool.

Although Minnesota has an international reputation for health care excellence, resources are not evenly distributed throughout the state. Rural Minnesota has a higher percentage of uninsured people than the rest of the state, and it has been faced with hospital closures and a loss of health care providers. In 1992, for example, the state reported 239 physician vacancies, the majority of which were in rural areas, and the closure of seven hospitals, six of which were in rural parts of the state. HealthRight addressed rural health care problems by creating an Office of Rural Health to improve health care planning and access. In addition, funds were made available to forgive state-funded loans to doctors, nurses and other midlevel practitioners who serve in rural areas, to increase the number of primary care residencies for medical students at the University of Minnesota and for those who will train in rural parts of the state, and to help financially troubled rural hospitals.

No portion of the Minnesota plan generated more political conflict than the funding proposal. Since I will discuss this issue below, I need only note here that the main battle was between advocates of an income tax surcharge (supported by health care providers, the hospital association, and certain key Democratic legislators, but vociferously opposed by Governor Carlson) and advocates of a 2 percent gross revenues provider/hospital tax. (A cigarette tax increase of 5 cents per package stirred little opposition and will be used for start-up costs and then transferred to the General Fund.)

The Minnesota HealthRight law is a highly complex and far-reaching achievement. It is the result of the efforts of some very skilled and astute politicians who were brought to the negotiating table as much by political circumstance as by policy commitment. It was their good fortune that predecessors had prepared the way to some degree.

PRELUDE TO REFORM

Minnesota's experience suggests that major health reform must be preceded by a period of statewide debate, education, and experimentation. Possibilities were discussed for more than a decade, during which time the state adopted some innovative measures and conducted several studies of its health care system and its needs. In the early years of this period, the focus was on access, especially for the uninsured, but gradually cost control dominated the debate.

Minnesota has the second-oldest state-run health care program in the nation, providing insurance for high-risk children and adults who, because of preexisting medical conditions, have been unable to obtain affordable coverage. Begun in 1976, the Minnesota Comprehensive Health Association currently enrolls 32,000 people who pay premiums that are partly subsidized by a tax on insurance companies.

HealthRight is the direct descendant of the 1987 Children's Health Plan (CHP). Initially CHP provided physician services for non-Medicaid eligible, low-income pregnant women, and children less than 6 years of age. The program was funded by a minimum annual fee ($35 for pregnant women, and $25 for children) and a cigarette tax of 1 cent per package. In January 1991 CHP was expanded to include all children through age 18. As one of the most successful and popular programs in the state, CHP provided a good administrative and political base on which to build HealthRight.

In the year before passage of the Children's Health Plan, the Department of Health sponsored a study of the financial problems facing the state's uninsured population. The result was a 70-page document called "The Challenge of Providing Financial Access to Health Care in Minnesota." It described the nature, scope, and consequences of inaccessible health care for low-income Minnesotans. The report recommended that the state expand Medicaid, preserve the charity system of care in the state and "establish a new managed, prepaid insurance program for the uninsured poor in the income range immediately above Medicaid."[8] The latter recommendation was given the name Healthspan to denote coverage that would "span the access gap" between those on Medicaid or other publicly subsidized insurance plans and those with employment-based insurance. The program would be administered by the Department of Human Services, which would contract with managed-care providers to offer services to the gap group.

At the same time that the Healthspan report was submitted (February 1987), Paul Ogren (DFL), became chair of the House Health and Human Services Committee. Ogren felt that the Healthspan report, which had almost immediately begun collecting dust, needed additional work. His committee secured a modest $45,000 appropriation to study health care reform. Ogren was convinced that more data were needed, and he contacted the United Way of Minnesota, the Children Defense Fund, and a Catholic health foundation to fund the hiring of a private law firm with actuary experience to conduct the study. The report was submitted to the Department of Human Services and became the basis for a Healthspan bill (House File [HF] 150) that proposed, among other things, a state-subsidized health insurance program for Minnesota's uninsured.

In 1989, however, the Minnesota legislature was not quite ready for major reform—and the new taxes it would require. In the end all the legislators could agree on was the creation of the Health Care Access Commission to undertake a review of health care access problems in the state, to "develop and recommend to the legislature a plan to provide access to health care for all state residents."[9]

The work and report of the Health Care Access Commission provided the genetic material for HealthRight. To begin, two members of the Gang of Seven, Senator Linda Berglin (DFL) and Representative Paul Ogren (DFL), were commission members, and the commission's extensive research provided much of the empirical basis for HealthRight. Because of the commission's work, Senator Berglin has said, "We probably have better information in our state about who the uninsured are, what their ages are, what their incomes are, and where they live, than any other state in the nation."[10]

The commission's proposals were broad and ambitious in scope. Briefly, it recommended that the state do the following:

1. Guarantee access to basic health care to all Minnesotans;
2. Subsidize the purchase of insurance for low-income people;
3. Require insurance companies to use community ratings;
4. Set statewide limits on health care spending;
5. Create reforms to control the administrative costs of insurers and providers; and
6. Consolidate the state's health care programs by creating a new Department of Health Care Access to improve administrative efficiency and service and reduce costs.[11]

The commission's recommendations were incorporated into a DFL-sponsored bill (Minnesotan's Health Care Plan or House File [HF] 2), with Ogren and Berglin again acting as key sponsors. The bill sparked an almost unprecedented lobbying effort, including the creation of a broad-based coalition of 30 groups called Minnesotans for Affordable Health Care (or, more simply, the Affordables). Supporters of HF 2 included health care providers (e.g., the Minnesota Medical Association, Public Health Association, Nurses Association), farmers' groups, religious organizations, labor unions, and social advocacy groups. Spearheaded by the Affordables, these groups sent out thousands of postcards and petitions, covered the state with lawn signs, buttons, bumper stickers, and billboards proclaiming "HealthCare for ALL Now!," held rallies across the state, and lobbied every state legislator.

It should also be noted that HF 2 had nearly unanimous editorial support throughout the state. This was in part due to the fact that the Health Care Access Commission had employed a public relations expert to work with editorial writers in the state. When HF 2 emerged out of the commission's work, it was both well known to and widely supported by the state's newspapers.

The educational, public relations, and legislative effort paid off when the Minnesota legislature passed HF 2 on the last day of the 1991 legislative session by comfortable margins, although largely along party lines, in both houses. The coalition supporting HF 2 then turned its attention to Governor Carlson, whose position was uncertain, although he was probably leaning toward a veto. The Affordables reminded the governor—and the people—that in his 1990 campaign he had promised, "My administration's targeted goal will be access to affordable health care for all Minnesotans."[12] But Governor Carlson was hearing from others as well: some Republican legislators, members of his staff, and representatives of the insurance and business communities were urging him to veto the bill. On 3 June the governor vetoed HF 2, charging that it was "budget busting," contained no cost-control provision, would increase insurance premiums for small employers and young people, and, perhaps most important, contained no long-term funding source.[13] Significantly, it was the absence of a funding mechanism that probably held together the coalition in support of HF 2. As long as no one—providers, employers, workers—was being asked to make any financial sacrifices, diverse support was easier to sustain.

In any event, the governor invited legislative leaders, as well as provider groups, insurers, and others, to develop "an affordable solution to the health care access problem." Carlson further stated, "Our collective charge will be first to fashion a responsible proposal that serves all of Minnesota's citizens well, a proposal that Minnesota taxpayers can afford." Interest and activity next turned to the prospects of a veto override. Supporters advocated the effort when the legislature returned, but the prospects were not promising: the bill had passed by eight fewer votes in the House than were needed for an override, although it was likely to succeed in the Senate. As legislative supporters contemplated their next step, an important chance meeting of personalities occurred.

HEALTH POLICYMAKING BEHIND CLOSED DOORS: THE GANG OF SEVEN

Anyone interested in health policy reform will find the process of policymaking in Minnesota at least as interesting and instructive as the substance of the reform. Even the participants in the process look back on the experience with amazement that so much was accomplished. The process in Minnesota may not be replicable, but it certainly offers one possible approach to building a consensus, sustaining political will, and handling pressure from interest groups.

In the fall of 1991 Minnesota politics hardly appeared conducive to a bipartisan approach to health care reform. Despite Governor Carlson's veto of HF 2, there were important political factors that were nudging the players toward reconciliation: the public wanted health care reform, the governor needed a political boost to revive his sagging popularity, and in 1992 the entire Minnesota legislature was up for reelection. As Dave Gruenes, a Republican member of the Gang of Seven, put it, "We realized that we needed each other; they had the votes, and we had the veto."[14]

The idea for reform occurred in the latter part of the summer of 1991, when Representative Ogren, a liberal Democrat, and Representative Gruenes, a conservative Republican, met at a chamber of commerce luncheon where they both were to speak on health care reform. Ogren, of course, was a key sponsor of HF 2 and chairman of the House Taxes Committees; Gruenes was a member of the House Health and Human Services Committee and chief spokesperson for the Republicans on health care issues. As the legislators listened to each other, they discovered that there was much on which they agreed. After the luncheon Gruenes suggested that they work together for reform. To Ogren, who was retiring from the House and anxious to end his legislative career with a successful health reform bill, Gruenes' overture was "marvelous." "It was the first time, in all these years of discussion and debate and legislation, that somebody from that side of the aisle had said, 'Look, there's probably some common ground.' "[15]

After the luncheon Ogren and Gruenes continued to meet and talk about general principles and problems. Both agreed that expanded access and cost control were interrelated and would be central to any plan. As the discussions proceeded they decided to bring in additional House colleagues. Each selected one other person to bring to the table. Ogren chose Representative Lee Greenfield, a liberal and an acknowledged expert on health care policy and especially health insurance. Greenfield headed the human resources division (i.e., the subcommittee) of the House Appropriations Committee, which would be needed for the passage of any health reform bill. Gruenes chose IR House minority whip Representative Brad Stanius, a pharmacist whose politics were quite conservative.

The four house members quickly concluded that consensus on reform was possible and that they would need the support of their Senate colleagues. The four became seven with the addition of the following: Senator Linda Berglin (DFL), chair of the Health and Human Services Committee and, along with Ogren, perhaps the most visible and experienced advocate of health care reform in the legislature; Senator Duane Benson (IR), Senate Republican leader, sponsor of Republican health care bills in 1990 and 1991 and indispensable to any bipartisan effort in the Senate; and Senator Pat Piper (DFL), advocate for low-income people and head of the health care access division of Senator Berglin's committee.

The bipartisan group consisted of seven well-placed and experienced lawmakers, each of whom was apparently committed to accommodation. Indeed, there was an explicit agreement that they would try to avoid the partisan one-upmanship typical of legislative sessions. The group agreed that none of the political parties, nor any individual, would take credit for the final product. Perhaps most important, each member agreed that once the group had reached consensus on a bill, they would stand together in defending all of it, even those provisions they might have previously opposed. Consequently, lobbyists would not be able to use a "divide-and-conquer" strategy. As Gruenes commented, "We were able to stand together, unified against any special interest groups with a vested interest in health care."[16]

The success of the group was due in part to personal relationships. Ogren and Gruenes were members of the same legislative "class" of 1980, and as Gruenes noted, "There's a certain amount of bonding that takes place when you go through the ranks together."[17] Although Benson and Berglin were not classmates, the two had a warm personal relationship, despite fundamental ideological differences. These personal relationships would help the group over some difficult periods in the course of their deliberations.

Let the games begin. The Gang of Seven began to meet formally in the latter part of November 1991. These meetings initially occurred about once a week, and then more often as the group approached the end of the process in early March 1992. Discussions often took place in an out-of-the-way Senate committee room, deliberately inaccessible to the media and interest groups. No one chaired the meetings, and no formal votes were taken. Agreement was reached by consensus. Representative Greenfield (DFL) commented, "If somebody vehemently objected [to a provision] you couldn't move on."[18] Staff members were asked not to speak with the media, lobbyists, or their colleagues on other committees; although inevitably some leaks occurred, lobbyists, legislators, and the media knew little about what was going on other than that the group was working on cost control, or insurance reform, and that they were making progress.[19]

Members began identifying those general issues and concepts that were essential to reform: cost control, expanding access to the uninsured (especially children), malpractice reform, rural health care problems, a health care access commission, and so on. Another important procedural decision helped facilitate accommodation of differing views. Gruenes had discussed his overture to the Democrats with Governor Carlson, who approved and promised to stay out of the process until a bill was ready. The governor's staff was kept apprised of the group's progress through the presence, at most meetings, of a health department staff resource person. The Carlson administration, however, made no effort to influence the process, nor was it encouraged to do so by the IR members.

In the first weekend in March word leaked out that the negotiators were close to an agreement. A bill would be drafted over the weekend and ready on Monday. What followed was a week of high tension and increased partisanship. At one point, in the words of one close observer, "It looked like the whole process was unraveling." The problem began when the draft that had been put together by staff over the weekend was reviewed by the Republican negotiators on Monday. The specifics of the draft's cost control provisions stunned the Republicans, who worried that a substantial new state bureaucracy would be created. In addition, the draft contained a certificate-of-need provision that they felt might stop, not merely slow, the introduction of new technology. The whole process was far more regulatory than the IRS wished it to be.

Moreover, the governor's office, which had obtained a copy of the weekend draft, was appalled by its contents. Curt Johnson, a staff person in the governor's office could not believe what he read was "anything that anyone with any conservative streak would have agreed to. The size of the implied bureaucracy was staggering." Another problem was that the draft proposed creating a health care commission and putting it *outside* the jurisdiction of the department of health, which meant that it was beyond the administration's control. After reading the bill, Mary Jo O'Brien, Deputy Commissioner of Health, concluded, "There is no way in hell that the governor is going to sign this bill."[20]

From Monday morning, 3 March, until well into the early hours of the following Monday, 10 March, negotiations between the governor's staff and the Gang of Seven went on almost continuously. In the end, the seven legislators were joined by administration officials. At this point it was clear that everyone wanted a bill. As one administration official put it, "The thing I remember most about that [Sunday night–Monday morning] session, other than its difficulty and occasional tension, was the increasing evidence that those [DFL] folks wanted a bill too. They wanted a bill more than they wanted an issue. And that was a critical turning point for me, and my willingness to continue to talk to the governor about it."[21] At 1:30 A.M. a compromise was reached. Six hours later the agreement was approved by the governor—although the bill was not yet in written form—and later that morning a celebratory news conference, with the governor, staff members, legislative leaders, and the Gang of Seven in attendance, was held announcing the compromise. The proposal was outlined in a document called "Health Reform for Minnesota: A Proposal by the Bipartisan Health Care Working Group." In essence the agreement closely resembled the final HealthRight law described above: a new insurance plan for the uninsured, modified community rating, various cost control measures, creation of an Office of Rural Health to implement reforms to improve the provision of health care services in rural areas, and funding through cigarette and provider taxes.

HEALTHRIGHT ON THE FAST TRACK: THE LEGISLATIVE PROCESS

The negotiators had five working days to move the bill through six policy committees (i.e., non-revenue/appropriations committees) and, in at least one chamber, to meet a deadline set by the legislative leadership. To expedite the process the legislators introduced three separately numbered but identical versions of the bill in each chamber, enabling simultaneous consideration by the different groups. One of these bills, having emerged in identical form from the three committees, would be sent to a fourth committee and constitute the House version. In another time-saving agreement, the legislative leadership of both parties agreed not to accept any amendments to the bill in the policy committees. The bill was introduced Tuesday, the day after the announced compromise, went to its first committee, the Senate Health and Human Services Committee, and was approved within hours of its introduction. (The Senate Health and Welfare Committee was chaired by Senator Linda Berglin.) The following day the bill cleared the House Judiciary Committee, again without amendment, and on Thursday it passed the House Financial Institutions and Insurance Committee and the Health and Human Services Committee. On Friday the bill passed its fourth, and final, House policy committee, Government

Operations. One lobbyist, reflecting on this period, recalls testifying before two or three House committees and not being asked a single question.[22] The bill moved equally quickly through Senate policy committees.

The opposition emerges. Once out of the policy committees, however, HealthRight ran into trouble. Interest groups knew little of the bill's content before its official unveiling. This, combined with the unprecedented speed with which it traveled through the policy committees, provided them with little time or information to respond to the proposal. By the end of that first week, however, certain key stakeholders were sufficiently educated about the bill and its implications to know that they did not like it. Thus, by the third week in March the process slowed down as opposition accelerated. What followed was "an awesome lobbying campaign. There were literally over a quarter of a million letters and faxes sent into legislators, driven by insurance agents, by the medical association, by the hospital association. The ferocity of the opposition really [couldn't] be exaggerated."[23] Foremost among the emerging opponents were elements in the provider industry, particularly the Minnesota medical and hospital associations.

During the weekend following the tumultuous first week of HealthRight's debut, the Minnesota Medical Association (MMA) leadership voted unanimously to oppose the bill. The association objected to the proposed spending limits on health care and limits on the acquisition and use of new technology and procedures, the prohibition of balanced billing for Medicare patients, mandatory participation in medical assistance programs, and restrictions on provider ability to refer patients to services in which they had a financial interest.

But particularly troubling to the MMA was the proposed 2 percent provider tax, which they characterized as "an inappropriate and unfair way of raising funds for this new program."[24] The physicians' association believed that program funding should be more broadly based so that everyone contributed to its support: "Just as Minnesotans share the cost of public education, so should all Minnesotans share financial responsibility for providing health care to those who can't afford it."[25] Supporters of the provider tax argued that revenues should be drawn from current health care expenditures and thus serve in part as a cost control mechanism. Furthermore, Republicans believed that there was more than enough money in the health care system to extend access to the uninsured and that the provider tax was the best way of redistributing that money. Finally, the governor was absolutely opposed to any increase of what was already one of the highest state income taxes in the country.

The MMA began a very aggressive lobbying effort against HealthRight. Some have charged that its campaign was unethical. Its most criticized facet was the solicitation of patient signatures on petitions opposing the law. The association sent out letters and petitions to 2,500 medical clinic managers, urging them to "counsel someone on your staff to work to obtain the signatures of patients."[26] Some legislators told of constituents reporting that they were urged to sign petitions while in examining rooms. The MMA denied the accusations; even so, it saw nothing wrong with asking clinic employees to solicit petition signatures in such spaces as waiting rooms.[27] But legislators were angered over this tactic and others. One event that particularly irritated legislators occurred on 31 March, when an estimated 450 physicians descended on the state capitol to express their views to the lawmakers. Legislators reported being angered by the arrogance of what they considered the self-serving interests of the physicians.[28] Many legislators, but especially key members of the Gang of Seven, including Ogren and Benson, publicly expressed anger at the physicians. Ogren, for example, pointed out that between 1985 and 1989 physicians' incomes grew, on the average, at a rate 24 percent greater than that of overall inflation. He protested, "I'm not against physicians earning a good living, but they should re-read their Hippocratic oath."[29] Benson began referring to the "medical-industrial complex."

The physicians were joined by the Minnesota Hospital Association (MHA), although the latter's opposition was not nearly as vehement. According to the chief lobbyist for the association, the MHA might have supported the bill if the legislature did the following: eliminated the mandatory Medicare assignment; modified, or better still eliminated, any certificate-of-need type of provision; and replaced the provider tax with a broad-based tax.[30]

Aside from these specific points, there was another issue that, according to John Kingrey of the hospital association, may have been MHA's most fundamental concern: "I think our priority is the government involvement in the running of health care, and what we saw as the potential for a single-payer system ultimately being accepted."[31] This fear was shared by others, especially those in the health insurance industry, another group that vehemently opposed the bill. Reacting to the HealthRight proposal, James A. Walter, the chairman of the Agents for Health Care Reform Coalition, observed to his members that "as the fine print was fleshed out, it became clear that the intent of this legislation was no longer to fine tune a private sector health care industry but rather to replace the current system with a single-payer system, much like Canada."[32]

Provider opposition to HealthRight was strongest and most vocal in rural communities. This was especially so among rural hospital administrators, who saw their existence threatened. The basis of this concern was twofold. First, the bill would exacerbate the already difficult task of recruiting and retaining physicians in rural areas. As one rural hospital administrator explained, the bill's provision to establish practice parameters "would affect Minnesota in general, but it's already very difficult in rural areas to recruit physicians. Some doctors are going to look at those practice standards and feel the state is taking away their autonomy."[33] Recruitment would also be made difficult because of mandatory Medicare assignment. According to Ken Banks, an administrator at rural Northfield Hospital, "Legislation which mandates Medicare assignment by all physicians and which will shift increasing numbers of people into a program [i.e., HealthRight] that reimburses providers at medical assistance rates will further damage physician recruitment in rural Minnesota to an extent from which it may never recover."[34]

Additionally, HealthRight's 2 percent tax might push financially troubled rural hospitals over the brink. It was in large part for this reason that the Minnesota Farm Bureau Federation, the state's largest farm organization, opposed the bill: "We have opposed the 2 percent tax on services of rural hospitals because we fear that this will in many cases serve to be the fatal blow to an already overburdened health care system in rural Minnesota."[35] Hospital administrators shared this view. As one rural hospital financial officer complained, "I hear Paul Ogren talking about the outrageous profits hospitals are making. I'd like to know where the heck those profits are. They're not in the rural areas."[36] Legislators from the rural areas spoke out in response. Senator Ron Dicklich (DFL) of rural Hibbing said, "Because it [HealthRight] has bipartisan support, everybody assumes it's a done deal. But the legislature is still controlled by rural people, and I don't think there's a lot of support right now for all the provisions of the bill."[37]

It should be emphasized just how powerful the provider industry is in Minnesota. Physicians throughout the country have long enjoyed extraordinary influence in state and national legislative processes, but Minnesota is a special case. The state prides itself on being a national, indeed an international, leader in health care. Perhaps the most visible symbol of that leadership is the Mayo Clinic of Rochester. The bargaining strength of the Mayo Foundation, the fourth largest corporate employer in Minnesota, was reflected in a letter from the president of the foundation to the seven legislative negotiators:

> Mayo is a significant stakeholder in this legislation. This bill as presently drafted will without doubt make it extremely difficult for Mayo to continue to compete nationally with other major medical centers. An exemption from the health planning provisions will make it easier for Mayo to continue to compete.
>
> The Minnesota economy benefits greatly from Mayo's status as a leading referral center. It is estimated that Mayo Rochester brought in $737 million in out-of-state revenue in 1990. This has been equated to hosting seven or eight Super Bowls each year. Mayo is one of Minnesota's largest employers with 17,629 employees.[38]

Although not every hospital or health provider has the clout of the Mayo Foundation, the health care industry was a formidable opponent.

Not all members of the provider community opposed HealthRight. Most notably, support came from the Minnesota Council of HMOs, representing ten HMOs with over one million members. In addition, an ad hoc coalition of providers was formed in support of HealthRight and included the Minnesota Chapter of the American Academy of Pediatrics, along with state associations representing nurses, psychologists, chiropractors, public health workers, mental health professionals, and the community health clinics. The Providers' Alliance to Show Support (P.A.S.S.) joined with more than 70 other labor, educational, social advocacy, religious, and philanthropic organizations lobbying on behalf of HealthRight.

On 4 April, when the Human Resources Division of the House Appropriations Committee voted to remove the temporary ban on new medical technology, a provision that physicians and hospitals had vehemently opposed. This victory was short-lived because it had come on an amendment by Representative Greenfield, Gang of Seven member and chairman of the Human Resources Division of the Appropriations Committee, who, in an abrupt about face, quickly withdrew the amendment, thereby nullifying the vote. The brief success was a harbinger of future difficulties for the HealthRight bill: providers and rural interests were their message getting through to the legislators.[39]

Soon opponents to the bill rolled up significant victories in the House. On April 8th, the full House Appropriation Committee eliminated most of the new technology controls from the bill, and the following day the House Tax Committee, on a close vote, dealt the bill a nearly fatal blow by dropping the provider tax and replacing it with an income tax surcharge. This was significant because the change both undercut one of the major provisions of the bill and threatened the bipartisan coalition that had forged it.

Republican negotiators were angry at both the provider lobby and Ogren, their negotiator with Democratic members of the house. Ogren chaired the House Tax Committee, and although he actually voted against the surtax, Republicans accused him of betrayal, believing that he had not successfully resisted pressure from physicians and hospitals. Some observers of state politics have contended Ogren apparently let it be known that he would not hold it against any colleague who voted for the income tax surcharge. If he did do so, he had two reasons: first, he was aware of the pressures legislators were under, especially those from rural districts; second, the vote did not make a difference since the provider tax would in any case be reinserted at the conference-committee stage, where the Gang of Seven would have a clear majority.

Whether or not there is any truth to this story, Republican negotiators were furious with Ogren. Benson said of him, "I thought we had a deal that we wouldn't cave in to everyone who wants to change the system." Benson also lashed out at the providers: "We're going to prove in this state . . . that the medical-industrial complex does not control Minnesota. People still control this state."[40] One of the main dangers of the change was that Governor Carlson was unalterably opposed to an income tax increase. Curtis Johnson, one of the governor's emissaries to the Gang of Seven, declared that the Tax Committee's action was "a vote to kill the bill."[41]

In addition to the squabbling over the tax and technology votes, another bit of news proved disquieting. George Hoffman, the head of the reports and forecast division of the Human Services Department, reported that the plan to cover the uninsured would cost, by 1997, not the originally estimated $200 million per biennium, but rather $540 million, and could reach $1 billion by the end of the decade. The new estimate had two immediate consequences. First, the Health Policy Coalition, a group of more than two dozen prominent business organizations, withdrew its support for HealthRight. Second, the House Tax Committee voted to scale back enrollment and reduce state subsidies to the plan for the uninsured.

At the same time, HealthRight's trip through the Senate was met with less opposition. The bill passed unscathed in the policy committees and in the Taxes and Tax Law Committee. It then went to the Finance Committee, which, much like its counterpart in the House, removed the technology controls and eliminated a one-year moratorium on new equipment and capital purchases (the latter change was intended to prevent a mad rush of purchases before controls could be put in place). Mindful of the new cost estimates, the committee changed the waiting period from four months to one year before persons without insurance could become eligible for coverage. The bill passed the Finance Committee and was sent to the Senate, where it was approved 48–18.

On 11 April the House voted 76–58 to approve HealthRight, with 69 Democrats and 7 Republicans in favor and 49 Republicans and 9 Democrats opposed. Despite an attempt by Ogren to have the House to overturn his own Tax Committee's decision, which was for the health tax, the House rejected it. The bill would now go to a ten-member House-Senate conference committee to resolve the differences; all the members of the Gang of Seven were on the conference committee.

The bill goes to conference. In a review of the differences between the House and Senate versions of HealthRight (HF 2800), a Senate Counsel reported to the Senate Conferees that "most of the differences are due to technical and clarifying changes that were not adopted in both houses. The difficult issues relating to the tax and HealthRight eligibility requirements represent only about 5 percent of the language."[42] Some technical points were, nonetheless, consequential. For example, the Senate version of HealthRight (SF 2603) used the term "limits" in various sections of the bill dealing with cost containment, while the House used the term "targets." Nevertheless, the critical sticking points involved the financing provision (which was debated by supporters of the provider tax and by those supporting an income tax surcharge) and the eligibility provision. An agreement was hammered out over two long days, primarily because all the conferees recognized that this was a bill that required a decision.

The financing mechanism was certainly the most difficult obstacle to overcome. The conferees had a difficult choice: accept the income tax surcharge and face an almost certain veto by the governor, or accept the provider tax and face possible defeat in the House, where that option had been overwhelmingly (91–42) defeated a few days earlier. The Gang of Seven, who were a majority of the conferees, were committed to supporting their original agreement; that meant a provider tax. This gave the Senate conferees an upper hand since their version, including the provider tax, came closer to the original bill. Yet there was considerable concern that the House conferees, and ultimately the full House, would not compromise on the issue. In addition, some House members calculated that the governor, despite his threats, would not, indeed politically could not, veto a health reform bill no matter how much he opposed its funding source.

Ultimately, the senators prevailed, and the real question became, What could be done within the conference to make a provider tax more palatable to the House? The answer was threefold. First, they agreed that the health care commission would review the provider tax after one year to determine whether it was the appropriate one for funding the program. Second, the conferees sought to assuage the concerns, particularly strong among House members, about the potentially mammoth costs of the program by making changes to control costs. (This was accomplished by scaling back the program in terms of benefits: a $10,000 limit was placed on inpatient hospital services. According to legislative staff estimates, about 85 percent of hospital admissions incurred expenditures under $10,000.[43])

Third, the conferees decided to limit eligibility to the HealthRight insurance plan. One of the main reasons for the recent upwardly revised cost of the program was the prediction that many buying insurance as individuals would leave that market and enter the less costly, state-subsidized program. The conference significantly reduced that possibility by requiring people to be uninsured for four months and without employer-provided insurance for 18 months before being allowed to enter the state plan. In addition, the conferees imposed a six-month state residency requirement for coverage and prohibited people from coming to Minnesota just to enter the program.

Three additional changes, appeared to be aimed at physicians, perhaps in the hope of reducing their opposition. These were a phase-in of the mandatory Medicare assignment over five years, the elimination of a felony penalty on the conflict-of-interest restrictions (i.e., physicians making referrals to services in which they have a financial stake) and the substitution of a $1,000 fine as punishment, and the elimination of a certificate-of-need approval provision and the substitution of one that required providers to inform the Department of Health when they make major purchases.

HealthRight becomes law. The compromise bill now went back to both houses, where typically conference committee reports are approved routinely. However, only five days earlier the House had overwhelmingly rejected a provider tax. Additionally, the bill's prospects had not been helped by an early, and potentially fatal, defection. Republican representative Stanius, who had been a helpful, if often reluctant, member of the original Gang of Seven, did not sign the conference report and called the governor to tell him that he would not support the compromise on the House floor. According to Stanius, the governor "went ballistic."[44] Carlson's main concern was that the Democrats might not have enough votes to carry the bill and that Stanius's defection would discourage other Republicans from voting for HealthRight. He also apparently wanted the bill's passage to look like a genuinely bipartisan effort, which, given the paucity of Republican support (only seven House Republicans and ten Senate Republicans had voted for the original bill), took some imagination.

The compromise reached the House on 15 April, where an emotional debate ensued. The roll was called, and a problem emerged. Those voting "Yes" numbered 62, 6 short of the majority needed for the bill's passage. At this point House Speaker Dee Long (DFL) stopped the vote board clock to allow the leadership of both parties to round up the necessary majority. Speaker Long called Governor Carlson and asked him to send over aides and to telephone Republican House members on the floor. The board was kept open while DFL leaders and Gang of Seven members, as well as the governor's staff and IR leaders, searched for additional votes. After 65 minutes the clock was restarted, and 8 additional votes were registered in favor of the bill. The House passed HealthRight on a vote of 70–64: 17 Republicans, 10 more than had voted for the original House version, and 53 Democrats, 16 fewer than had supported the original bill, voted in favor of the measure.

Republicans are convinced, and some Democrats have admitted, that the DFL had the votes to pass HealthRight without additional Republican support: the party leadership could have gotten between 10 and 20 more DFL votes in favor of the bill if it wanted them. The DFL leaders, however, wanted to give some of their members from rural districts a chance to avoid their constituents' ire by voting against the bill. As it turned out, more than 85 percent of those who voted against HealthRight came from rural Minnesota. To do this, some Republican votes for the bill were necessary.

Shortly after the House action, the Senate, in much less dramatic fashion, overwhelmingly approved HealthRight after only brief debate.

CONCLUSION

HealthRight or, as it will now be called, MinnesotaCare, will not lead to universal access to health care for all Minnesotans, at least not by the end of this century. Current projections estimate that it will cover about 40 percent of the uninsured in the state by 1997; this scenario reflects the financial limitations of the state. Nor was it possible at the time to completely impose community rating; only gender-based rating is prohibited, although bands are set around other rating factors. Similarly, the state did not seriously confront medical malpractice reform and delayed, perhaps for a year, an effective effort to curb spending on high-cost technology. Each of these shortcomings were realistic compromises that Minnesota lawmakers had to make to win legislative and executive approval of their reform. In the end, the instructive value of the Minnesota experience lies not in the remaining imperfections of the reform law, but in the story of how state officials were able to accomplish as much as they did, given the formidable obstacles to reform.

Was the extraordinarily cabal-like approach of the Gang of Seven necessary, or could reform have proceeded more openly? This is a question of some interest, given the controversy over the secret deliberations of Hillary Rodham Clinton's national task force on health care. For Gruenes, the answer was clear: "Could the process have been more open? Perhaps. Would we have been successful? I rather doubt it."[45] The private negotiations of the Gang of Seven protected them from the party, as well as legislative-executive, conflicts that had caused the stalemate over HF 2. Greenfield commented, "Who said what to who, who said what about what, was to be kept private. This is what led us to be able to find out what we agreed on. It would've been impossible in a formal [i.e., open committee meetings] context."[46] The explicit decision by the governor to stay informed but to remain outside the process until a proposed package was ready, and the implicit decision by the negotiators that this was not going to become a partisan issue, gave reform a chance. During the negotiations these seven legislators developed an esprit de corps and a sense of ownership of the emerging bill. Their camaraderie was fostered in part by the group's procedural decision that once they reached an agreement on a particular provision they would all stand by that decision, regardless of their party's position.

All seven legislators held some position of formal authority (e.g., committee or subcommittee chairman, minority leader, etc.) or brought to the process an understanding of health care policy. This enabled the negotiators to control the process through a focused understanding of the issues. Although health care was not a traditionally Republican issue, the months of private negotiations leading to the introduction of HealthRight helped the IR negotiators in working quickly when necessary and prepared them for dealing with their colleagues.

The decision to isolate health reform from routine partisan and infragovernmental branch bickering enhanced the prospects of its success. This approach, however, had mixed results with regard to interest-group politics and the ultimate outcome. For the Gang of Seven, one of the virtues of secrecy was that the group would be insulated from pressure. They would decide who would know what and from whom they would solicit information. The negotiators could take this approach in part because they were not dependent on interest groups for information. Health reform had been so highly discussed in recent years that the group had about as much information on the various issues as the lobbyists. Their knowledge freed them from the influence peddling that is the implicit quid pro quo in legislative-interest group information exchanges.

By not having to rely on lobbyists, or even to keep them informed, the group had, of course, another tactical advantage. As one negotiator said when the bill was finally made public, "We did take them by surprise."[47] It took lobbyists nearly a week to launch a counteroffensive, and by then the bill had cleared every House policy committee and some of the Senate committees as well. And it did so without any significant changes. One lobbyist, a former state legislator who was both sympathetic to the cause of reform and critical of the process, admitted, "If this thing had been done by the normal process, you [the interviewer] wouldn't be here. There wouldn't have been a thing done. . . . I think in terms of good government. I think it's [i.e., the secrecy of the negotiations] a real dangerous way to do business, but it was the only way this thing was going to happen."[48]

Those who did not support HealthRight, however, were less generous in their assessment of the process. Representatives of the provider groups used such phrases as "knifed in the back," "like Eastern Europe before the fall of communism," and "left out" when describing the process of the bill's passage and their treatment. One official of the Minnesota Medical Association portrayed the process as "pretty foreign to the way politics is carried out in this state. . . . This was no longer a discussion. They went behind closed doors. They did dirty politics."[49]

The important point, of course, is not to judge retrospectively how closely the process conformed to democratic theory, but what its implications are for implementing reform. Physicians, or at least those who share the position of the MMA, remain estranged from and bitter about both the process and its outcome. Many are convinced that the provider tax and mandatory Medicare assignment will discourage new physicians from practicing, and established physicians from staying, in Minnesota. Some doctors have even suggested that the law cannot work without the providers' support and that such support may not be forthcoming. Interestingly, providers opposed to the law favor about 85 percent of what is in it. The parts they are most opposed to have to do with their income.

Why were Minnesota's lawmakers so successful in resisting the "medical-industrial complex," given its reputation for effective lobbying? Much of the answer has already been provided. First, Minnesota medical and hospital associations were kept in the dark until very late in the process and had to scramble about in their lobbying efforts. Second, some of their tactics antagonized many lawmakers. Third, the medical establishment did not speak with one voice on this issue: most notably, HMOs and Blue Cross-Blue Shield were supporters of HealthRight. Fourth, because much of the providers' opposition revolved around money issues and the bill's impact on their incomes, a number of legislative and advocacy supporters of HealthRight were able to portray the health care providers as self-serving. "What it looked like was that they [the providers] were more concerned about how much money they earned than they were with what was going to happen to people who didn't have health care; and they didn't come out looking very good."[50] Finally, the health care professionals did little to dispel this impression or to communicate the fact that they supported the vast majority of the bill.

The normally powerful provider lobby was defeated by the necessity of change. In Minnesota, health care reform was simply an issue that could not be ignored. Reform in Minnesota was driven by the public expectation that something needed to be done about controlling the costs of care and expanding patient access. Additionally, legislators were concerned that any party appearing to obstruct reform would pay the political price. Once state Republican leaders supported the bill—and they had to travel a good deal of political distance to do so—reform took on an air of inevitability that apparently the provider industry did not appreciate or fully understand.

The above circumstances may explain why once the actual implementation of the law began, the physicians and hospitals abandoned their opposition and decided to try to influence, not merely oppose, the process. Beginning in the summer of 1992, the Health Care Commission and, then later, the legislature worked on cost control. That process, now with provider support, continues today.

1. Although I will use the terms "Democrat" and "Republican" in this paper, the actual titles of the two parties in Minnesota are the Democratic-Farmer-Labor Party (DFL) and the Independent Republican Party (IR). Minnesotans seem somewhat casual in their usage, sometimes referring to Democrats and Republicans and at other times to DFLers and IRs.
2. Minnesota state officials learned in July 1992 that they could not use the name HealthRight because a California company has held a trademark on the name since 1977. The program has subsequently been renamed MinnesotaCare.
3. *Grand Forks Herald*, 8 March 1992.
4. The Minnesota Health Care Access Commission, *Final Report to the Legislature* (January 1991): 4.
5. State of Minnesota, HealthRight Law, Chapter 549, Article 1, Section 1.
6. The Minnesota Health Care Access Commission, *Final Report to the Legislature* (January 1991): 4.
7. Ibid.
8. Minnesota Department of Health, Office of Health Systems Development, *The Challenge of Providing Financial Access to Health Care in Minnesota* (February 1987): 42.
9. Minnesota Health Care Access Commission, *Final Report to the Legislature* (January 1991): 2.
10. Author's interview with Senator Linda Berglin (DFL), 11 August 1992, hereafter referred to as Berglin interview.
11. Minnesota Health Care Access Commission, *Final Report to the Legislature* (January 1991): 5–6.
12. From a flier entitled "Governor, You Promised," supplied to the author by John Clawson, past president of Minnesotans for Affordable Health Care.

13. Veto message of Governor Arne Carlson, 3 June 1991.

14. Author's interview with Representative Dave Gruenes (IR), 13 August 1992, hereafter referred to as Gruenes interview.

15. Author's interview with Representative Paul Ogren (DFL), 10 August 1992, hereafter referred to as Ogren interview.

16. Gruenes interview.

17. Gruenes interview.

18. Author's interview with Representative Lee Greenfield (DFL), 10 August 1992, hereafter referred to as Greenfield interview.

19. A statement typical of the media's lack of knowledge was the following from an editorial in the *Star Tribune*, ". . . word has leaked out that while the negotiators are hitting hard on containing medical costs—bless them—they are having difficulty developing a means to finance care for Minnesotans who now don't have it." *Minneapolis Star Tribune*, 23 February 1992.

20. Author's interview with Mary Jo O'Brien, Deputy Commissioner of Health, 14 August 1992.

21. Author's interview with Curt Johnson, Assistant to the Governor, 13 August 1992.

22. Author's interview with John Kingrey, senior vice president of the Minnesota Hospital Association, 14 August 1992, hereafter referred to as Kingrey interview.

23. Ogren interview.

24. Minnesota Medical Association, letter to Senator Linda Berglin, 19 March 1992.

25. *Lafayette-Nicollet Ledger* (Nicollet Co., Mn.), 2 April 1992.

26. Minnesota Medical Association, memorandum to "Clinic Administrator Legislative Network and Calling Tree," 19 March 1992.
27. For a contrary view from some medical ethicists in Minnesota, see *St. Paul Pioneer Press*, 2 April 1992.
28. See *Minneapolis Star Tribune* 1 April 1992.
29. *St. Paul Pioneer Press*, 31 March 1992.
30. Kingrey interview.
31. Kingrey interview.
32. James A. Walker, chairman, Agents for Health Care Reform, "Legislative Alert," 24 March 1992.
33. *Hibbing Daily Tribune*, 18 March 1992.
34. Ken Bank "HealthRight Racing at Unhealthy Speed," *Northfield News*, 1 April 1992.
35. Al Christopherson, president of the Minnesota Farm Bureau Federation, letter to members of the Senate Finance Committee, 6 April 1992.
36. *Hibbing Daily Tribune*, 18 March 1992.
37. Ibid.
38. Robert R. Waller, M.D., president of the Mayo Foundation, letter to the Gang of Seven, 18 March 1992.
39. See *Minneapolis Star Tribune*, 4 April 1992.
40. *St. Paul Pioneer Press*, 9 April 1992.
41. *Minneapolis Star Tribune*, 9 April 1992.
42. Michael Scandrett, Senate Counsel, memorandum to Senate Conferees on HF 2800, 13 April 1992.
43. *St. Paul Pioneer Press*, 16 April 1992.
44. Author's interview with Representative Brad Stanius (IR), 11 August 1992.

45. Gruenes interview.

46. Greenfield interview.

47. Berglin interview.

48. Author's interview with John Clawson, executive director, Community Clinic Consortium, 12 August 1992.

49. Author's interview with Dr. Stuart Hanson, president elect, Minnesota Medical Association, 12 August 1992.

50. Berglin interview.

Rationing Care in Oregon: The New Accountability

Daniel M. Fox and Howard M. Leichter

The Oregon Basic Health Services Act became a projective test for the national media and many health policy experts soon after it became law in July 1989. Proponents praised its boldness: for the first time in the United States, they said, elected officials, community leaders, and health professionals were defining an adequate minimum standard of health care for a substantial number of people. Rationing of health services for some of the poor and for the uninsured had become, in Oregon alone, a public process that was based on expert analysis and opinion and the discussion of community values. Moreover, the priorities recommended by experts in the context of community values are subject to the vote of the legislature. Opponents of the Oregon program complain that it is unfair to poor women and children, who will be the first to experience explicit rationing, and that it oversimplifies the problems of assessing the effectiveness of medical care.

In this article, we describe the politics and policy of the Oregon rationing plan. We neither attack nor defend the Oregon program. Our purpose is to place it in context: to explain why problems that have been politically salient in every state—namely, rising Medicaid costs and lack of access for the uninsured—are being addressed differently in Oregon.

Our thesis is that the events in Oregon occurred mainly because health professionals who had positions of authority believed that these problems could be solved by reason, frankness, and good will. These beliefs made it possible for a plan conceived in order to ration services to become, gradually, a guarantee of a minimum set of medical services, initially for the poor. The people who created and are implementing the Oregon plan assume that the problems of cost and access can be solved by community discussion, by applying to policy research-based knowledge about assessing opinions and values and weighing the costs and benefits of medical intervention, and by legislative decisions that are accountable to the voters. These assumptions politicize the ideals of many health professionals. Reason, frankness, and good will are synonyms for competence (and belief in ever-advancing technology), compassion (expressed as concern for patients' autonomy and comfort), caring, and accountability.

Many health professionals in Oregon have expressed unusual public concern about health policy and how it is made. The legislative sponsor of the Oregon plan was a physician. In community meetings convened across the state to assign value to health services, most of the participants were health professionals, as are seven of the eleven members of the Health Services Commission, which ranked thousands of medical procedures. The leadership of health professionals has not been the whole story in Oregon, but it is the major story.

What has been described as unique to Oregon is that many health professionals and the legislature seem to have accepted public responsibility to ration services. But health professionals everywhere routinely make judgments about the appropriateness of alternative technologies in the context of the needs and resources of their patients. When resources are scarce, as they almost always are, health professionals everywhere allocate them on the basis of these judgments. But they rarely (bolder historians would say almost never) make rationing decisions in public, rarely make them about populations rather than about individuals, and rarely do so in coalition with other leading citizens—and especially not with legislators. Making decisions about what to ration in Oregon has, not surprisingly, also led to a unique consensus about what medical services people should expect to receive.

EXPANDING ACCESS AND RATIONING CARE

Oregon's Basic Health Services Act explicitly confronts two of the most critical challenges facing the nation's health care system: guaranteeing access to health care for all Americans and containing the growth of health care costs. To accomplish these seemingly contradictory goals, Oregon is trying to ration health care through an accountable political process rather than by the decisions of individual providers or by actions of state government that change eligibility for services or coverage in response to strains on public budgets. The state has defined a minimum entitlement to basic health services and is applying it initially to certain limited groups, excluding persons covered under Old Age, Blind, and Disabled; Medically Needy; and Children in Foster Care programs.

Leaders in the legislature, however, want the entitlement to apply to the entire population. In addition, supporters of the plan reject critics' accusation that Oregon will finance coverage to the uninsured only by cutting services in current programs. "Nothing could be further from the truth," say the sponsors. "[T]he state intends to put more state general fund dollars into Medicaid. . . . No state budget is exempt from the potential of being reduced in order to provide additional funding for the Medicaid program."[1] Although national attention has focused on only one part of this effort—rationing health care for Medicaid recipients—the Oregon plan involves three related pieces of legislation, each dealing with a different population: those on public assistance, uninsured workers, and the medically uninsurable population.

Expanding eligibility levels. The centerpiece of the plan is Senate Bill 27, or the Oregon Basic Health Services Act. Under the law, everyone who falls below the federal poverty level is eligible for health care through the Medicaid program; previously, only those with incomes of 58 percent or less of the federal poverty level were eligible for Medicaid in Oregon. Expanding access to an additional 160,000 Oregonians would, of itself, substantially increase the state's health care bill. Hence, there would have to be a trade-off between access and benefits to control costs. As explained by State Senator John Kitzhaber, the architect of Oregon's new health plan, "If we can agree that society cannot afford to buy everything [in health services] for everyone who might conceivably benefit from it, then we have to develop a process to determine what level of care everyone should have access to."[2] In other words, health care must be rationed.

Reallocation of resources. To ensure the "social and political consensus" that Kitzhaber and others believe is vital to the success of the policy, an elaborate mechanism has been designed to allocate health resources. The law creates an 11-member Health Services Commission to conduct public hearings and encourage public involvement in preparation for recommending a prioritization of health services. The commission is to submit its recommended priorities to the governor and a Joint Legislative Committee on Health Care by 1 July of the year preceding each regular legislative session. Accompanying the list of priorities will be a report by an independent actuary on the rates for each of the services/treatments. The Joint Legislative Committee on Health Care will recommend to the full legislature whether to accept or reject the commission report. Should the legislature accept the report, it must then decide how much it is willing to spend on health care for the next biennium. This money will then be used to buy a package of health services for each recipient from as far down the priority list as the legislative allocation will allow.

Should a revenue shortfall occur, or should the number of persons below the poverty level increase, the state cannot drop people from the program or reduce payments to providers below the cost of providing services "without compromising quality."[3] Instead, the legislature will retreat back up the list of priorities until it reaches the point at which there is enough money to provide services for all those eligible under Medicaid. This provision helps to explain the support for the plan from many leading providers in the state, including the Oregon Medical Association, Oregon Association of Hospitals, and health maintenance organizations (HMOs) such as Kaiser Permanente.

Reimbursement. The legislation establishing the plan guarantees that reimbursement will be negotiated after careful analysis, rather than established arbitrarily and then cut in response to state budget problems. Moreover, the legislation promises to reward the largest and most efficient Medicaid providers (including those called "disproportionate share providers") and to squeeze those who are inefficient or simply greedy. Finally, by denying reimbursement for specific uncovered services, the plan would discourage anyone from providing them to Medicaid-covered or uninsured patients and would, logically, abolish below-cost reimbursement for them. As a result, cost shifting would be eliminated in Oregon for the covered populations. The loss of the ability to shift costs (valued by hospitals, disdained by payers) may account for some of the "serious reservations" that, according to the Senate president and his staff, some providers expressed initially about the plan.[4] (Other reservations involved providers' fear of losing clinical autonomy and of the erosion of existing mandates for private insurance coverage.)

Once the budget and priorities are agreed on, the state's Department of Human Resources will negotiate prepaid, managed health care service contracts with hospitals, HMOs, physician care organizations, and managed care plans. The law provides for exceptions to the prepaid managed care approach in some rural areas.

Increased access to care. In addition, Senate Bills 534 and 935 apply the principle of expanding access to two other groups of Oregonians. The first consists of about 10,000 to 20,000 people who are considered uninsurable due to preexisting medical conditions. SB 534 creates an insurance pool from which these people can purchase health insurance. Although the original legislation does not extend the concept of a basic level of services found in SB 27 to this group, the plan is to do so in the next legislative session.

The more important of the two bills is SB 935. This is aimed at working Oregonians and their dependents who are above the federal poverty level but who have no health benefits and do not qualify for medical assistance. The law affects about two-thirds of the uninsured in Oregon (approximately 300,000 people). Under this legislation, employers are encouraged, through tax credits, to provide health insurance for uninsured employees. Significantly, the law provides that the benefits offered to these employees "must include substantially similar medical services as those recommended by the Health Services Commission [under SB 27]." Although SB 935 initially applies only to businesses with 25 or fewer employees, the legislature is authorized to extend the provision to all employers.

Universal coverage. From the outset of the legislative process, Kitzhaber portrayed the benefits package created by SB 27 as a standard for a minimal level of health insurance coverage for all Oregonians, even for the nation. Kitzhaber believes that no one should be outside the "health care lifeboat"— one of his favorite metaphors. On this point there has been both confusion and disagreement. Although Kitzhaber's belief in the universality of the legislation has been evident from the outset, it was not shared by other participants in the legislative hearings on SB 27. For example, when one witness in the early stages of consideration of the bill suggested that SB 27 "sets up a minimal acceptable level of health benefits and implies that all businesses in Oregon must provide at least that level of benefits," she was corrected by a committee member who said that he did not interpret the bill to mean that at all. The benefits that employers provide to their employees are the result of contract negotiations, he noted, not state policy.[5] As late as April 1989, after the bill had been approved by the Oregon Senate, another lobbyist argued before the House Committee on Human Resources that "when you develop the list [of health priorities] in Senate Bill 27, that list, as a result of other legislation [Senate 935], also becomes potentially the definition for adequate health care for both your employed, uninsured, and your employed insured. *And this is not something that I think is widely known.*"[6]

Not only was it not widely known, but some of those who were aware of the broader implications of SB 27 were troubled by them. The lobbyist for the Oregon Chapter of the National Association of Social Workers, for example, was concerned that extending the minimum standard established in the law to all Oregonians would lead to a leveling down of benefits to an "admittedly inadequate level" for most Oregonians.[7] Only after SB 27 became law and critics such as Rep. Henry A. Waxman (D-CA) and Sen. Albert Gore, Jr. (D-TN) began attacking it as "unfair" to the poor did supporters begin emphasizing the not "widely known" point about its relevance to all Oregonians, and not just the poor. On 11 April 1991, Kitzhaber introduced a bill to establish a Health Care Purchasing Authority, which would require insurance carriers to offer the Basic Health Services Plan to companies and individuals, even to companies that self-insure.

However broadly or narrowly one chooses to define or understand the implications of Oregon's package of health insurance legislation, it is bold in both concept and prospect. How is it that Oregon took on the role of health policy innovator in this instance? The answer to that question lies in both a common malady that afflicts all the states and a particular expression of that problem in the state of Oregon. We begin with the more general affliction.

MEDICAID: 'THE MONSTER THAT ATE THE STATES'

Although no sector of the health care economy has been immune from the escalation of costs, the public sector has been especially hard hit. Government spending accounts for a substantially larger portion of the health care bill today than it did 25 years ago: 26.2 percent in 1965 and 41.4 percent in 1987. Private spending over this period increased by 848 percent; public-sector spending by 1,784 percent, mainly as a result of the introduction of Medicaid and Medicare in 1965. Medicare accounts for over 80 percent of federal spending on health. Medicaid has become, in the words of former Oregon Governor Neil Goldschmidt, "the monster that ate the states."[8]

Medicaid is second only to education in the percentage of state budget it consumes and second only to corrections in rate of growth over the past decade. When it was first introduced, Medicaid consumed about 5 percent of state general fund expenditures; today the figure is about 11 percent and is predicted to go as high as 15 percent by 1995.

The growth in Medicaid costs has a good deal to do with trends in the coverage of the two major groups in the program, persons who receive Aid to Families with Dependent Children (AFDC) and Supplemental Security Income (SSI). Eligibility for AFDC has become more restrictive and that for SSI, more expansive.[9] As the number of AFDC recipients, especially children and single (often female) parents has been reduced, SSI payments for older and disabled persons have kept pace with inflation since payments are indexed to the cost of living. Between 1975 and 1985, overall benefit levels for AFDC recipients declined 30 percent, while those for SSI and state-provided supplementary income (SSP) recipients increased 10 percent.[10] This has meant that the number of younger people eligible for Medicaid declined, while the number of older people increased. In 1988, about 70 percent of the Medicaid population were children, but they received only 12 percent of money spent on the program, while 73.4 percent went to SSI recipients. In 1972, in contrast, 18.1 percent of Medicaid expenditures went to AFDC-eligible children and 52.8 percent to people on SSI.[11]

State responses to Medicaid growth. In response to the growth in Medicaid spending, the states have adopted one or more of three strategies. All three are, in effect, methods of rationing the consumption of health services. The first two ration by eliminating coverage or beneficiaries; the third, by creating disincentives for providers to treat. One strategy has been to eliminate certain benefits, as Oregon did in 1987 when it ended state funding of organ transplants. Second, states have redefined eligibility and consequently thrown people off the Medicaid rolls. As a result, the proportion of poor people in general who are covered by Medicaid has declined from a high of about 65 percent to less than 40 percent today.[12]

Third, states have reduced reimbursements to providers—a strategy rendered more difficult by a June 1990 U.S. Supreme Court decision that upheld the right of hospitals and other health providers to sue the states for higher Medicaid reimbursements. In 1989, for example, Oregon reimbursed hospitals for only 78 percent of the actual cost of providing services under Medicaid. Oregon was one of the states in which a lawsuit by providers seeking increased reimbursements was pending when the court issued its ruling.

Medicaid trends in Oregon. Oregon Medicaid trends mirror those at the national level, with one exception. Oregon's program is unique in a way that helps to explain support for the managed care emphasis of the Basic Health Services Plan: an unusually large number of Oregon Medicaid recipients (55 percent) are currently in managed care programs. Between 1979 and 1989, overall federal and state expenditures for Medicaid in Oregon increased by 83 percent, and the cost per recipient increased by 69 percent. However, those eligible for the program increased by only 8 percent during 1979–1989. Between 1979 and 1985, persons in the program actually declined by 17 percent—from 139,918 to 116,614. Only in the 1987–1989 biennium, following an improvement in the state's economy and nationally mandated expanded eligibility, did the number of Oregon Medicaid recipients exceed the 1979–1981 level.

THE TRANSPLANT CONTROVERSY

The specific personal experiences of Oregon policymakers transformed these statistical trends into innovative policy change. The death of a seven-year-old boy from Portland set the stage for health care rationing in Oregon. Like many other states, Oregon first authorized funding of transplant operations under Medicaid in the 1983–1985 biennium legislative session. In the first two years of the program, requests for transplant funding were approved case by case. The state could reject any transplant request and could stop the program when it had exhausted the allocated funds. In 1985, however, Congress required that states file a plan indicating which procedures they would fund. They were then obligated to fund all transplant requests that fell under the plan.

In 1987 the Oregon Department of Human Resources requested $2.2 million from the legislature to cover 34 transplants, an increase of $1 million over the previous biennium. The Human Resources Subcommittee of the House and Senate Ways and Means Committee decided to take transplant funding out of the regular budget and place it on an optional priority list, along with other requests for special social programs. The subcommittee had about $20 million at its disposal; requests totaled about $48 million. The transplant program had to compete with programs dealing with the mentally ill and disturbed, the deaf, head injury victims, juvenile delinquents, and senior citizens. The subcommittee ran out of money before it was able to face the issue of funding transplants.

Prenatal care was not, however, one of the competing priorities. Much would be made later on by the national media and legislative leaders about how Oregon had eliminated organ transplants for a few individuals to spend those dollars on prenatal care for many more women. The state did increase funding for prenatal care during the session, but that decision was made by another subcommittee and was unrelated to the transplant decision.

The decision to eliminate transplant funding was hardly noticed by the legislators. State Representative Mike Kopetski, who introduced the Human Resources budget, called attention to the deletion of the transplant program twice in his speech. Not a single legislator questioned the decision.[13] The next transplant decision, however, drew the attention of the nation upon the state. Medicaid officials told the unemployed and uninsured mother of Coby Howard, the seven-year-old with leukemia, that her son could not receive a bone marrow transplant. The boy's family, friends, and teachers had organized a private fund-raising campaign, which was $30,000 short of its $100,000 goal when the little boy died on 7 December 1987.

Coby Howard's death and the existence of five other uninsured transplant candidates resurrected the transplant issue. In a January meeting of the Legislative Emergency Board, which acts on behalf of the full legislature during the interim period, Rep. Tom Mason introduced a motion to appropriate $220,000 to the state's Medicaid program to fund five transplant operations for people whose requests for such procedures had already been denied. The proposal was opposed by Oregon Senate President John Kitzhaber, who presided over a subcommittee meeting on the proposal on 28 January 1988. He and House Speaker Vera Katz took the unusual step of attending the subcommittee meeting to vote on the funding request.[14] Kitzhaber said that the issue before the Emergency Board was not whether the state could find $220,000 to fund these five requests. Clearly it could. He argued, however, that the "basic issue is one of equity." Thousands of working Oregonians had no private insurance, and still other nonworking Oregonians were ineligible for Medicaid. Neither of these groups were eligible for these transplants. "I think what this [transplant] policy does," Kitzhaber said, "is it gives to Medicaid recipients certain services that are not, in fact, available to a large number of other Oregonians. . . . [T]here's a basic inequity involved there. What you're really doing is you're asking many taxpayers to buy services for people on public assistance that they can [not] even get for their own children."[15]

Another critical issue was one of priority. Since a state cannot satisfy all demands, it has to make choices on how best to spend its dollars. "What we can do with our limited money is to reduce the number of deaths to the maximum. Save as many people as we can, because we can't save them all," Kitzhaber said.[16] Despite an emotional plea by Representative Mason that Oregon not become "known as the state that lets children die," his motion failed on a tie vote. Kitzhaber and Katz voted against the motion.[17] The next day, however, the full Emergency Board was scheduled to meet, and Mason vowed to bring the issue before it.

That evening, Ted Koppel featured the Oregon transplant decision and Kitzhaber on "Nightline." He began the program with footage of Coby Howard and said: "When the State of Oregon decided to stop funding organ transplants, it allowed this boy to die." Koppel later asked: "Is the cost of modern medical technology forcing public officials to play God?"[18] It was in the rather heady atmosphere of national media attention, then, that the full Emergency Board met the next day. The arguments about equity, priorities, costs, and compassion were the same; so were the results. The motion was defeated. In the course of the debate, Kitzhaber set the stage for the next act in this drama: "Now I guess I just want to close by saying that we are going to have to ration health care."

WHY OREGON?

In his closing pronouncement, Kitzhaber meant explicit, systematic rationing, not what had long been occurring in Oregon and elsewhere. In his view, the decision to halt funding of transplants was an exercise in rationing health care one procedure, even one patient, at a time. That the Coby Howard decision became the occasion for a much larger debate can be attributed not only to the highly publicized, specific tragedy involved, but to the political and social culture of Oregon and to John Kitzhaber himself. Oregonians, ever mindful of the history of the Oregon Trail and of courageous pioneers, take pride in their innovative social policy. More recently, *The Almanac of American Politics* described Oregon as "a culturally liberal state on many issues, with many young and single voters, and one that is proud of being the first state to ban throw-away bottles and among the first to allow abortions."[19] The popular image that Oregonians have of themselves has been called a "moralistic" political subculture, in which "both the general public and politicians conceive of politics as a public activity centered on some notion of the public good and properly devoted to the advancement of the public interest."[20]

Political circumstances also contributed to the ability of the state to tackle the difficult policy issue of rationing. Democrats controlled both houses of the legislature and the governorship, and the leaders of the two houses were close friends and political allies. Kitzhaber, who was first elected to the Oregon House in 1978 and has been in the Senate since 1981, has served three terms as Senate president. His experience as an emergency room physician has added credibility to his role as the premier legislative authority on the state's health policy system and has aided him in gaining support within the medical community. Although Kitzhaber had been better known for his interest in environmental than in health issues, once he assumed the position of spokesperson in the transplant controversy, he pursued the issue of resource allocation with enthusiasm. His articulateness and personal warmth have helped him assume national celebrity status since Oregon first made the news with its decision on transplants.

Kitzhaber remained the dominant force in formulating the new health policy partly because Governor Neil Goldschmidt decided that he had other priorities. In February 1988, at the time the Emergency Board was embroiled in the transplant controversy, the governor appointed an 18-member Commission on Health Care, which he charged with "identifying Oregonians who find it difficult to gain access to health care." The commission members came largely from the health field, including the presidents of the Oregon Medical Association, Blue Cross/Blue Shield of Oregon, and the Oregon Health Sciences University. In September 1988, the commission recommended encouraging business to use an existing voluntary tax credit program to cover uninsured employees, creating an insurance risk pool, and extending Medicaid benefits to pregnant women.[21]

Although some commission recommendations found their way into the Basic Health Services law, the report had only a minor impact because the governor did not promote it.[22] Some have suggested that the governor was preoccupied with other policy interests, including prison finance and his "Children's Agenda"; others have suggested that he was simply uninterested in health care reform. Thus, SB 27 was, in every sense of the term, "Kitzhaber's plan." He had the power, the allies, and the idea.

RATIONING HEALTH CARE

Senate Bill 27: the legislative route. Kitzhaber's dominance was both facilitated and symbolized by one of the first tactical steps he took in preparation for the legislative debate on his bill, namely, the creation of a new Senate Committee on Health Insurance and Bioethics. This move enabled him to bypass the existing Human Resources Committee and its less congenial chairperson and deal instead with a sympathetic freshman senator, Bob Shoemaker, who, in addition to being an attorney and ally of Kitzhaber's, had served as counsel to the Multnomah County Medical Society.

Although SB 27 underwent several revisions, there was little dispute from critics to health providers over its fundamental assumption that the current system was unsustainable and that rationing was unavoidable. Ken Rutledge of the Oregon Association of Hospitals stated, for example, that "major reform of our current health care delivery system and payment system is needed."[23] Three committees conducted hearings on the bill between February and June 1989. In February, Kitzhaber said the bill was a "mere skeleton," really just a "concept." The skeleton was fleshed out as House and Senate committees heard testimony from health care providers and insurers, business leaders, social advocacy groups, union leaders, business leaders, and members of public health and welfare bureaucracies.

There was a good deal of disagreement about particulars. The most consequential concern, and the one that would become the rallying point later for opponents both in the state and in Congress, was over the trade-off between access and benefit levels. Central to Kitzhaber's plan was the notion that not everyone would be able to get all the medical care they might want or need. About 400,000 Oregonians neither qualified for Medicaid nor were covered by private insurance. Any coverage at all would be more than they currently received. But universal access would have to come at the cost of limiting health services both to those on Medicaid and to those with private insurance for whom SB 27 might provide a standard of coverage. Since neither the government nor the private sector could afford unlimited health services to everyone, the state would define an adequate or basic level of health services. But critics wondered if the benefit package that emerged from the process would in fact be adequate. Some who testified indicated that although they supported universal access, if presented with a choice between a "thin" package of benefits for everyone and something short of universal access but with more substantial coverage, they would prefer the latter. In addition, some charged that the plan would create a two-tiered health care system: guaranteed access to limited services for the poor and virtually unlimited services for those who could afford to purchase insurance on their own.

As a result of these concerns, opponents wanted some assurance that the basic benefits package would be rich enough to provide an acceptable level of health care. This view was summarized by Ellen Pinney of the Oregon Health Action Council, a coalition of more than 70 groups representing labor, senior citizens, minority groups, and low-income people. "I think all of us remain somewhat uncomfortable with passing a bill of this magnitude through the legislature without defining, in very clear terms, what the benefits plan will look like," she said.[24]

Legislators themselves did not know precisely what the package would include. That decision would be made by the legislature after the Health Services Commission completed its work of "rank-order[ing] health services according to their benefit to the entire population being served." However, the legislature did vote to "maintain the status quo in the Medicaid program until there was a new benefit package for them to review."[25]

Providers were also concerned about the adequacy of the benefits and reimbursement under the plan. For example, Kaiser Permanente, one of the largest HMOs in the Northwest and a major Medicaid contractor, said that it might not bid on the program at all because it would either lose money or offer inadequate benefits.

It soon became clear that the legislature would have to address the uncertainty about benefits. Under pressure from lobbyists, the House Human Resources Committee amended the Senate version of the bill to include a broad definition of basic health services. This included "so much of each of the following as are approved and funded by the Legislative Assembly: (1) Provider services and supplies; (2) Outpatient services; (3) Inpatient hospital services; and (4) Health promotion and disease prevention services." The list apparently reduced some of the concerns surrounding the bill.

Many providers began to claim access to the system for their specialties. Dentists, drug and alcohol counselors, mental health specialists, social workers, pharmacists, chiropractors, and osteopaths, among others, pressed to make certain that their services would be included in the package authorized under the law. The earlier versions of the bill had prohibited any reduction in reimbursement without a corresponding reduction in the services they were required to provide. In April 1990, this language was changed to require that the state pay the rates necessary to cover costs of services as determined by an independent actuary.[26] To providers who knew other states' Medicaid reimbursement policies, the bill would now appear to be almost a model of fairness, even if they risked having all or some of their services excluded from the benefit package.

The membership on the Health Services Commission was also a matter of some debate, as both provider and community groups sought representation on the commission. Ultimately, the bill stated that the commission would consist of eleven members, five of whom would be physicians with clinical expertise in the areas of obstetrics, perinatal care, pediatrics, adult medicine, geriatrics, or public health. One of the physicians would be a doctor of osteopathy; in addition there would be a public health nurse, a social services worker, and four "consumers of health care."

The law required the commission to "solicit testimony and information" from groups that did not have direct representation. The groups specified included advocates for seniors; handicapped persons; mental health services consumers; low-income Oregonians; and providers of health care, including but not limited to physicians licensed to practice medicine, dentists, oral surgeons, chiropractors, naturopaths, hospitals, clinics, pharmacists, nurses, and allied health professionals. The legislators were eager to secure widespread support for the plan. Supporters of the bill frequently used such phrases as wanting Oregonians to "buy into the reform" and to have a "sense of ownership." Moreover, as Kitzhaber and his staff recall, it was "important to know what consumers wanted out of the system."

To construct the broadest possible support base for the program, and also mindful of the severe public criticism that followed the death of Coby Howard, the bill included a charge to the Health Services Commission to solicit the views of the general public and thereby help "build a consensus on the values to be used to guide health resource allocation decisions." This would occur in a series of community meetings around the state.

Finally, the legislative committees adopted several changes to deal with potential problems for providers and consumers in a health system based on legislated rationing and managed care. Hospitals and physicians were protected from malpractice suits resulting from their inability to provide services not authorized under the law. Also included was a provision to inform patients about any treatment or services that they might need but that are not covered under the program.

SB 27 was approved with overwhelmingly bipartisan support in both houses of the Oregon legislature after extensive debate, especially in the Senate. The law was approved by a margin of 19 to 3 in the Senate and 58 to 2 in the House.

Setting priorities. Two very difficult tasks lay ahead before the state could implement the Oregon Basic Health Services Act. The first was to obtain Medicaid waivers from the federal government. The second task was for the Health Services Commission to construct a list of health service priorities for the legislature.

To accomplish their task, the Health Services Commission used three formats, two of which were mandated by the law. The first was a series of 11 public hearings held around the state allowing interested parties to express their views. The second was to authorize Oregon Health Decisions (OHD), a highly respected citizens' advocacy group, to conduct community meetings in every county of the state "to build a consensus on the values to be used to guide health resource allocation decisions." Ultimately, 47 of these community forums were held, during which participants filled out a questionnaire soliciting their opinions on the relative importance of certain health situations and categories, engaged in group discussions, and viewed a slide show. Health care interest groups dominated this stage, as they had in many points of the process.

Although it was the hope and intention of OHD to attract a cross section of Oregonians, this did not turn out to be the case. Of the slightly more than 1,000 people who attended the meetings, almost 70 percent were mental health and health care workers.[27] Although the term *workers* is not defined, it should be noted that over one-third of the participants had incomes of $50,000 or more, and two-thirds were college graduates. Kitzhaber is convinced that the "discussions were wide-ranging and tended to deal primarily" with broad issues and values rather than with narrow interests. The attendance at the meetings and accounts of the discussions suggest that a substantial number of Oregon providers were comfortable enough with the plan to want to help shape it.[28]

The third mechanism provided the most systematic solicitation and application of citizen values in the prioritization process. The commission authorized a statewide, random-digit-dialed telephone survey of 1,000 Oregonians. To conform to the principle of incorporating community values in the ranking process and not simply relying on treatment and outcome data, the commission decided to use a modified version of the Quality of Well-Being Scale developed by Robert M. Kaplan of the University of California at San Diego. Respondents were asked to rate 31 health situations from 0 (a situation that is "as bad as death") to 100 (a situation that describes "good health"). Among the situations respondents were asked to rate were the following: "You cannot drive a car or use public transportation, you have to use a walker or wheelchair under your own control, and are limited in the recreational activities you may perform but have no other health problems," and "You can go anywhere and have no limitations on physical or other activity, but wear glasses or contact lenses."[29]

The results of the survey were then formally incorporated into a mathematical cost/utility or "net benefit value" formula that included data on expected outcomes of given treatments for hundreds of health conditions. The "net benefit value" equation was in the form of a word formula where net benefits equal net benefit value divided by net costs. Benefits included the length of time the patient benefits from a treatment, the public values regarding certain health states (for example, death, return to asymptomatic state of health, and so on), and the probability that a state of health will result from a particular treatment. Costs include diagnosis, hospitalization, professional services, nonmedical but prescribed services, and ancillary services.[30]

The formula produced a computer-generated prioritized list of 1,600 condition/treatment pairs. The first version of this list was released 2 May 1990 by the Health Services Commission and received widespread national media attention.[31] Data collection and methodological problems gave the list some rather surprising priorities: crooked teeth received a higher ranking than early treatment for Hodgkin's disease, and dealing with thumb sucking was ranked higher than hospitalization of a child for starvation.

Members of the commission insist that the initial prioritization was never intended to be anything more than a test of the methodology. In August 1990, Commission Chair Harvey Klevit told a reporter for the journal *Science*, "I looked at the first two pages of that list and threw it in the trash can."[32] The commission created an Alternative Methodology Subcommittee to rework and modify the original formula. On 20 February 1991 the Health Services Commission made public a "Prioritized Health Services List." The list, which was considered preliminary, awaits an actuary's pricing of each of the 800 health services and treatments identified before submission to the legislature in April 1991. The committee chairman noted that there may be "as much as 5 percent variation between" this list and the one reported to the legislature.

The comments accompanying the list made it clear that the commission relied more heavily on negotiations—in their words, on public values and clinical judgment—than it had in the first exercise. As commission member Tina Castanares, a physician, said on behalf of the commission in a statement accompanying the list, "Our own values and judgments . . . prevailed . . . where we felt that the other methods fell short."[33] An interview in March 1991 with Amy Klare, one of the four consumer representatives on the commission, confirmed the view that the list was the product of intense negotiation among members. One widely debated issue, for example, was the relative priority assigned to various preventive medical and dental services. While some members of the commission, including Klare, felt that the high value assigned to preventive services by Oregonians in the community forums dictated that such services receive a high priority, some of the physician members were less convinced about the relative utility of, say, nutritional supplements and dental check-ups. In the end, however, the force of expressed community values prevailed, and preventive health services received a high priority on the list.[34]

The resulting list contained over 700 rather than the original 1,600 medical conditions and treatments. This scaling down was largely accomplished by grouping related treatments, such as open fractures of the toe, ankle, and lower leg, into broader categories, such as fractures of the lower extremities. In addition, the end result was a far more rational, and presumably medically and politically defensible, product. There are 17 major categories, ranging from "acute fatal, prevents death, full recovery" (for example, various forms of pneumonia) to "fatal or nonfatal minimal or no improvement in QWB" (for example, "terminal HIV disease with less than 10 percent survival rate at five years"). From the perspective of the history of SB 27, among the more interesting changes between the two lists is the relocation of organ transplants from near the bottom of the original list to various locations throughout the revised list, depending on an assessment of potential outcome.

THE FATE OF THE OREGON EXPERIMENT

The fate of the legislation depends, as it has from the outset, on factors both within the state and in Washington, D.C. The Health Services Commission created its priority list. The legislature then considered the plan in May and June 1991, after the actuary provided a cost list for each treatment. By then, two new political factors had complicated the process. The first was that Republicans regained control of the Oregon House in November 1990 (though Kitzhaber remained Senate president—for one lame-duck session—with a larger Democratic majority). The second factor was that in the same election, Oregonians approved a property tax limitation that strained the state's budget, especially as it tried to compensate for shortfalls in local expenditures for education.

On 19 August 1991 Oregon requested that the federal government waive certain Medicaid laws so that it could implement a demonstration project built around the principle of universal access to a basic package of health care services for the poor. State officials could pursue two routes: convince officials in the Department of Health and Human Services (HHS) to grant the waiver, or get legislative authorization for the waiver. In 1989 the Senate Finance Committee, on which Sen. Bob Packwood (R-OR) is the ranking Republican, voted to grant a waiver.[35] However, it was dropped from the budget bill by the Senate Budget Committee.[36] State officials then gave priority to securing an administrative waiver. They were encouraged in this effort by what they interpreted as support from Gail Wilensky, then Health Care Financing Administration (HCFA) administrator and soon after a White House policy adviser.[37]

The plan drew more attention in April 1992, when the Congressional Office of Technology Assessment (OTA) reported that for those who were ineligible for Medicaid in Oregon the "implications of the new eligibility and coverage rules [under SB 27] are unambiguously good." The OTA concluded that current Medicaid beneficiaries "would both gain and lose something under the proposed plan." The OTA also had reservations about the "lack of any minimum level below which benefits may not fall."[38] By late April state officials, and Wilensky herself, were predicting that a decision from the Bush administration was imminent.

But opponents now became more vocal. Rep. Henry Waxman (D-CA), for example, wrote to HHS Secretary Louis Sullivan that he found "offensive . . . a government rationing proposal that affects only low income families."[39] Groups in the state that had initially opposed the plan, including the Oregon Catholic Conference, Oregon Fair Share, and the Oregon Human Rights Coalition, renewed their criticism.

The White House, especially Wilensky, now criticized the plan. In June 1992 the Office of Management and Budget (OMB) announced that no decision was imminent. Observers in the state and the national media attributed the delays and Wilensky's backpedaling to Bush administration reluctance to endorse a "rationing" plan during a presidential campaign.

The Americans with Disabilities Act (ADA) of 1990 presented an unexpected new obstacle. In late July 1992, 20 national organizations representing persons with disabilities publicly urged President Bush to reject the waiver request because the Oregon plan violated the ADA. On 3 August Secretary Sullivan informed Oregon Governor Barbara Roberts that he would not grant the waiver because the state's plan was in conflict with the ADA. In particular, the statewide telephone survey in which Oregonians rated various health situations with regard to their impact on a person's quality of life was "based in substantial part on the premise that the value of life of a person with a disability is less than the value of life of a person without a disability."[40] According to informed sources, the decision had actually been made in the White House, under the strong influence of C. Boyden Gray, the president's counsel and an ally of interest groups on behalf of disability rights.

The secretary's decision enraged the plan's supporters. Oregon State Senator John Kitzhaber called it a "disgusting performance," and Senator Packwood declared that "we have been betrayed."[41] Defenders of the plan reminded critics that Oregonians were surveyed about the impact of various health conditions on the quality of their own life, not that of others.

Sullivan had, however, "urge[d] Oregon to submit a revised application which addresses these [ADA] concerns."[42] This message was reinforced by HHS officials; at the end of August they told commission members that if references to "quality of life" were taken from the prioritization process, "you have a very high likelihood of approval."[43]

State officials decided to prepare a revised list immediately, rather than awaiting the outcome of the 1992 presidential election. In their new waiver request, submitted ten days after Bill Clinton was elected, the HSC made three major changes to the prioritization process and subsequent list: it eliminated the survey results and judgments about quality of life from the new prioritization; it shortened the list from 709 to 699 condition/treatment pairs; and it placed greater weight on the judgment of the commissioners in assigning ranks.

CLINTON TAKES OVER

The day before Bill Clinton's inauguration, a Bush political appointee in the Justice Department wrote to HHS that the revised plan continued to have "features that violate ADA."[44] This parting shot, soon leaked to disability rights advocates, became a source of new attacks on the Oregon plan.

The HSC accorded highest priority to treatments that would "return the patient to an asymptomatic state of health" after saving his or her life. Justice charged that the designation "asymptomatic" denigrated the quality of life of persons with disabilities.[45] *Symptom,* as defined by Oregon, was apparently another term for *disability.*

The memorandum from the Justice Department amplified the initial HHS rejection that able-bodied citizens tend to devalue the lives of the disabled. Infertility services had low ranking because "they are not highly valued by Oregonians," the HSC wrote. But infertility, Justice said, was a "disability within the meaning of the ADA."

Meanwhile, Oregon officials believed that President Clinton would be more sympathetic to their request. Candidate Clinton had endorsed the plan in May 1992 and again in the second presidential debate in October. When members of the Oregon congressional delegation, including Rep. Ron Wyden (D), Packwood, and Sen. Mark Hatfield (R), met in late January with Donna Shalala, the new secretary of health and human services, she was well informed, generally sympathetic, but noncommittal.

Senator Hatfield forced the administration's hand, after Oregon leaders told him that a waiver decision was needed quickly so that the legislature could fund the plan in the 1993–1995 state budget. Hatfield announced in mid-February that unless the administration made a prompt decision on the waiver, he would attach an amendment to a National Institutes of Health (NIH) authorization bill stipulating that if the waiver decision was not made by 19 March 1993, it would automatically be deemed approved. On 17 February 1993 Shalala told Hatfield that she agreed to the deadline.

In mid-February Hatfield and state officials learned of the 19 January Justice Department memorandum. The Clinton administration may have wanted to ignore the objections raised by Bush's Justice Department, but disability advocates obtained and leaked to the press a copy of the memorandum. Intense consultations then occurred between HHS and state officials. On 12 March, one week before the decision deadline, a group that included Secretary Shalala's chief of staff, head of intergovernmental relations, and two HHS attorneys made an unpublicized trip to Salem, Oregon. In a day-long session with the governor's staff (and, briefly, Governor Roberts), the Oregon Department of Human Services, and the HSC, these officials tried to reach agreement on changes in the waiver request.

State officials believed that HHS was "looking for a way to make this thing work," despite their concern about political embarrassment from legal challenges to the list and the methodology on which it was based.[46] State negotiators shared this concern, but they were reluctant to make more pragmatic adjustments on the list of priorities.[47] In addition, state officials worried that the HSC commissioners would rebel at yet another request for revision.

The HHS negotiators tried to address the 19 January memorandum by urging that the priority accorded to achieving "asymptomatic" status be replaced by the commissioners' judgment of "medical effectiveness." In addition, the HHS officials wanted the state to modify the low ranking of infertility. Two days later the state negotiators reported that the HSC had agreed to change the methodology and revise the list as a condition for obtaining the waiver.

State and federal officials immediately began negotiations on proposed terms and conditions to accompany the waiver. Simultaneously, 70 advocacy groups urged President Clinton to reject the Oregon plan. Newspapers reported that Vice-President Al Gore was going to meet with the president to reiterate his earlier opposition. Rumors circulated in Washington that the strong ties between the Children's Defense Fund and the administration would prevent the waiver's approval.[48] But on 19 March Secretary Shalala approved the waiver for a period of five years. "The President," she wrote to Governor Roberts, "believes that the Federal Government must give States the flexibility to design new approaches to their local problems, provided these proposals meet Federal standards."

Implementation of the Oregon Health Plan was now contingent on state compliance with 29 terms and conditions outlined in a memorandum accompanying Shalala's letter to Roberts. Most important, the state had 60 days to "re-rank the condition/treatment pairs without relying on data which it collected with respect to whether treatment returned an individual to an asymptomatic state."[49] Moreover, although the state was not required to include infertility services at all, the rank of this condition had to be based on "content neutral factors that do not take disability into account." Finally, the state had to adopt guidelines for health providers to minimize the likelihood that someone, particularly a disabled person, would be denied care if they had an eligible condition.

CHANGING LANDSCAPE IN OREGON

When prospects improved for the Oregon plan in Washington, they became worse in Salem. Oregon government was in crisis as the result of a 1990 property tax limitation initiative estimated to produce a $1.2 billion state deficit in the biennium beginning 1 July 1993. The state will need an estimated $83.6 million in state funds to pay for the basic health benefit package (as it stood 19 April 1993) to go into effect 1 January 1994. If the state does not find the revenue, the list of 565 covered treatments must be cut, which would require federal approval. If funding is not forthcoming, state officials say, the plan will not be implemented. The state's political landscape has changed since the Oregon plan was adopted. In 1989 Democrats controlled both houses of the state legislature, as well as the governorship. Senate President John Kitzhaber and House Speaker Vera Katz were powerful allies. Both have since left the legislature. Moreover, the Democrats lost control of the House in 1990 and emerged from the 1992 elections with a slim majority in the Senate. No one has yet emerged to fill the leadership void Kitzhaber's departure created.

In addition, bipartisan support for the Oregon plan is eroding. The Republican House Majority Speaker, for example, did not join the governor in the press conference announcing the waiver approval (although he says he supports the plan). One-third of the members of the 1993 Legislative Assembly have no personal investment in or experience with the plan.

The weakening of legislative support is exacerbated by an apparent disarray of allies outside the legislature. At the beginning of the 1993 legislative session, Governor Roberts proposed raising most of the funds to implement the health plan through a health provider tax—1.5 percent on gross hospital revenues and 0.9 percent on physicians and dentists—and from increased cigarette taxes. Both proposals are opposed by such original supporters of the health plan as the Oregon Medical Association (the provider tax) and the Association of Oregon Industries (AOI) (both taxes).[50]

The AOI, the state's major business lobby, has become the most serious obstacle to the plan's implementation. The organization accused the state of reneging on two promises. The plan, it says, was to be financed through general funds, not special taxes that could be passed back to employers as higher insurance premiums. Moreover, the AOI asserts that the waiver conditions prevented the state from reducing the basic benefit package, which is inconsistent with the law's original intent that the state adjust benefits in line with its financial status.

Most important, the AOI may be retreating from the mandate because of its increasing numbers of members from small business.[51] The original law provided that once the waivers were obtained to cover the Medicaid population, employers would be required, by July 1995, either to offer their employees a benefit package substantially similar to that established by the HSC or to pay into a state insurance pool fund, which would be used to subsidize alternative insurance for uninsured workers and their dependents. Small-business leaders and some legislators worry that after the play-or-pay mandate goes into effect, some low-wage employees will be shifted from Medicaid to employer-provided or subsidized insurance, thus putting a new financial burden on small businesses. The state believes that this reflects the original intent of the law and will also help to reduce Medicaid case loads and to lower costs. The shift will, moreover, help meet a precondition of the waivers that "annual expenditures do not exceed pre-defined limits on the number of demonstration eligibles and costs incurred."[52]

Although rescinding the employer mandate would not invalidate the federal waiver, it would make staying within HCFA's expenditure caps difficult. Roger Auerbach, Governor Roberts's chief adviser on health care issues, says that maintaining the mandate is "a major policy issue because we need to hold everybody together in support of the plan if we are to achieve our goal of getting this Medicaid expansion financed."[53]

The Oregon Health Plan is seriously threatened, according to legislative leaders. Governor Roberts maintains that the state will find some way to raise the necessary revenue, but she has failed to persuade the legislature on other fiscal issues. A local journalist wrote that "we could be looking at a major anticlimax here."[54] But it is hard to imagine the state walking away from something that so many have struggled with for so long amid such intense national publicity.

LESSONS FROM OREGON

The employer mandate covering working Oregonians currently without health insurance takes effect 31 March 1997, for businesses with 26 or more employees; and 1 January 1998, for businesses with fewer than 26 employees. (In both circumstances this applies to employees who work more than an average of 17.5 hours per week.)

On 14 September 1993 Governor Roberts signed into law Senate Bill 5530 implementing the Oregon Health Plan. The law provided for an additional $65 million in state funds needed to extend health services to an additional 120,000 Oregonians not now covered by Medicaid. The additional funds are to come from General Fund dollars and a 10-cent-per-pack cigarette tax. Beginning 1 February 1994, Medicaid clients will receive a basic package of health services covering 565 of 696 treatments in the prioritized "List of Physical Health Services." Beginning 1 January 1995, these services will be expanded to include mental health and chemical dependency treatments. That benefit package will include 605 of 745 treatments from the prioritized "List of Integrated Health Services."

The innovation in Oregon is that leading health professionals, other community influentials, and the legislature have become publicly accountable for explicitly rationing services to the poor and the near-poor. This is a considerable achievement. But Kitzhaber and his staff assert that they have done more: Oregon is "hold[ing] society accountable for the rationing of health services to the poor through the legislature."[55] We do not find society's participation to be broad to date.

Kitzhaber and others also take issue with our finding that the assent and cooperation of providers, and especially of physicians, have been essential to the creation of the Oregon plan. They agree that "health care providers played a central role" in the "prioritization process." But they insist that the place of providers in decision making "was highly structured."[56]

In our view, medical professionals played a central role in the Oregon rationing decision for three reasons. Obviously, they enjoy structural advantages in any health policy debate: status, organization, knowledge, and resources. That they have been willing to use their resources to influence the political process in general is reflected in the fact that in recent years the Oregon Medical PAC has ranked among the top five political action committees in the state in terms of expenditures, and the "Health and Medical" lobby is among the top three in spending on legislative lobbying.[57] Second, they were well represented at critical stages of the process. The third reason is that while readers of *The New York Times* might well have concluded that rationing was the burning issue of the day in Oregon, readers of *The Oregonian* would not have reached the same conclusion. Rarely, if ever, during its legislative life was rationing a front-page story in the state's largest newspaper. Few people outside the social advocacy and health service provider communities either knew of or understood the potentially broader implications that Kitzhaber envisioned for his legislation. For the most part, it was a story about how people on Medicaid and other poor Oregonians would be guaranteed access to health services. It was certainly not an unimportant story, but neither was it apparently central to concerns of most Oregonians. In the absence of nonmedical popular or elite interest, the playing field was left largely to the medical experts.

Many informed cynics have complained that the Basic Health Services plan may never be extended beyond poor women, children, and persons currently uninsured. The more idealistic of these cynics charge that the result for the poor and the near-poor will be rationing without representation. This is hardly an innovation. Just as with medical dominance of medical decision making, taxpayers and their elected representatives have a long history of deciding how charitable they want or ought to be. Other critics of the Oregon plan charge that the technology for assigning priorities to particular treatments is badly flawed. But the technology that is, increasingly, being employed to set priorities in Oregon is one that has been used with considerable public support in this country for two centuries: bargaining among interest groups that makes use of the analysis and opinions of experts and is then ratified by legislative action.

Three lessons emerge from the Oregon experience. The first is that citizen participation was a legally flawed strategy to gain widespread acceptance for innovative reform. It may also have been flawed politically; unelected and therefore unaccountable persons who were predominantly white and middle-class were vulnerable to the critique that they set priorities for people they did not represent. The second is that specificity (the infamous "List") can become a political albatross. No state has emulated the list or seems likely to do so soon.

The final lesson of Oregon is ironic. As a result of debates about rationing, Oregon lawmakers backed into defining what is in effect a minimum basic package of services. In so doing, they showed that it is possible to design and implement a plan that puts a floor of coverage under everyone in the state.

ACKNOWLEDGMENTS

The preparation of this paper was supported by the Milbank Memorial Fund. The authors thank Sen. John Kitzhaber and his staff for extraordinary generosity in providing information and arguing with us. Mark Gibson was unusually forthcoming and cheerful, even when convinced that we were wrong. It will be obvious to readers, however, that our conclusions are very much our own. We also thank Jean Thorne and Lynn Read of the Oregon Office of Medical Assistance Programs and Ian Tim of Oregon Health Decisions.

NOTES

1. Oregon Senate President's Office, "SB 27 Issues and Responses" (Salem, Oreg.: May 1990), 1–2. Opponents of the program, particularly nationally and those in Washington, D.C., have criticized state officials for the initial focus on the most vulnerable populations, namely, women and children. However, our research provided convincing evidence that the reason for the initial limitation was tactical and administrative; the ambitious nature of the program and the difficulty in providing long-term care under Medicaid led to the exclusion of the other groups from SB 27. Persons in the Old Age, Blind, and Disabled and Foster Care programs will continue to receive benefits under existing Medicaid rules.
2. Testimony of John Kitzhaber, Oregon Senate President, before the Oregon House Committee on Human Resources, 19 April 1989.
3. Memorandum from John Kitzhaber and Mark Gibson to the authors, 26 December 1990.
4. Ibid.
5. Senate Committee on Health Insurance and Bioethics, 16 February 1989.
6. Testimony of Mark Nelson, National Association of Social Workers, before the Oregon House Committee on Human Resources, 19 April 1989 (emphasis added).
7. Ibid.
8. Quoted in T. Hutchison, "The Medicaid Budget Tangle," *State Legislatures* 16 (March 1990): 17.
9. See B.O. Burwell and M.P. Rymer, "Trends in Medicaid Eligibility: 1975 to 1985," *Health Affairs* (Winter 1987): 30–45.
10. Ibid., 32–33.
11. National Center for Health Statistics, *Health, United States, 1989* (Hyattsville, Md.: U.S. Public Health Service, 1990): 258.

12. See J. Rovner, "Medicaid: A Safety Net Riddled with Holes," *CQ Weekly Report* (20 February 1988): 366. Burwell and Rymer similarly document the erosion of Medicaid coverage of poor children. Burwell and Rymer, "Trends in Medicaid Eligibility," 34–35.
13. Author interview with former Oregon State Legislator Mike Kopetski.
14. Kitzhaber and his staff claim that Kitzhaber presided only because the regular chair, Frank Roberts, was in the hospital. Other sources insist, however, that his attendance at the meeting was quite unusual. Memorandum, 28 November 1990.
15. Transcript of Oregon Legislature Emergency Board, Human Resources Subcommittee, 28 January 1988.
16. Ibid.
17. Kitzhaber and his staff insist that he had "moved [unsuccessfully] that funding the transplant program be restored *and* that the funding for prenatal care be increased as well." The effect of this motion was to persuade "influential members of the committee" that it was necessary to "concentrate on accomplishing the greatest possible good." Memorandum, 26 December 1990.
18. "Nightline," 28 January 1988.
19. M. Barone and G. Ujifusa, *The Almanac of American Politics, 1990* (Washington, D.C.: National Journal, 1990), 1001.
20. D.J. Elazar, *American Federalism,* 3rd ed. (New York: Harper and Row, 1984), 115–122.
21. Governor's Commission on Health Care, "Report to Governor Neil Goldschmidt on Improving Access to Health Care for All Oregonians" (Salem, Oreg.: Office of Health Policy, 1 September 1988).

22. Office of Medical Assistance Programs, "Waiver Application for Oregon Medicaid Demonstration Project, Discussion Draft" (Salem, Oreg.: Department of Human Resources, 26 April 1990).
23. Ken Rutledge, Oregon Association of Hospitals, testimony before Senate Committee on Health Insurance and Bioethics, 16 February 1989.
24. Ellen Pinney Oregon Health Action Council, testimony before the Oregon House Human Resources Committee, 19 April 1989.
25. Memorandum, 26 December 1990.
26. Ibid. (The actuarial report was released 1 May 1991.)
27. R. Hasnain and M. Garland, *Health Care in Common: Report of the Oregon Health Decisions Community Meeting Process* (Portland, Oreg.: Oregon Health Decisions, 1990), 29.
28. Memorandum, 26 December 1990.
29. For a copy of the complete questionnaire, see Health Services Commission, "Preliminary Report" (Salem, Oreg.: 1 March 1990), Exhibit 2.
30. Health Services Commission, "Preliminary Report," 1 March 1990, Exhibit 5.
31. *The New York Times*, 3, 6, and 12 May 1990.
32. V. Morell, "Oregon Puts Bold Health Plan on Ice," *Science* (3 August 1990): 468.
33. T. Castanares, "Statement on Behalf of the Oregon Health Services Commission upon Release of the Prioritized List of Health Services, 20 February 1991.
34. Author interview with Amy Klare, 18 March 1991.
35. M.C. Kimball, "Fluid Odds on Oregon's Medicaid Waiver," *Health Week* (11 March 1991): 12.

36. A.K. Ota, "Oregon Health Plan May Get Grease," *The Oregonian*, 9 April 1992, C9.
37. U.S. Congress Office of Technology Assessment, *Evaluation of the Oregon Medicaid Proposal* (Washington: U.S. Government Printing Office, May 1992), 1.23–42.
38. *The Oregonian*, 11 April 1992, A1, A14.
39. Rep. Henry A. Waxman (D-CA), as quoted in M. Abramowitz, "Oregon Blazes a Trail," *The Washington Post*, 9 June 1992, Health Section.
40. *The Oregonian*, 4 August 1992, A1, A8.
41. Ibid.
42. *The New York Times*, 4 August 1992, A8.
43. *The Oregonian*, 27 August 1992, C4.
44. Letter from Timothy Flanigan, assistant attorney general, Office of Legal Counsel, Department of Justice, to Susan Zagame, acting general counsel, Department of Health and Human Services, 19 January 1993.
45. Oregon Health Services Commission, *Prioritization of Health Services, 1991*, Appendix D, D-23.
46. Authors' interview with Lynn Read, Oregon Health Plan, 21 April 1993.
47. Authors' interview with Jean Thorne, Oregon Office of Medical Assistance Programs, 6 April 1993.
48. The Children's Defense Fund (CDF) has been one of the most vocal and active critics of the Oregon plan. During the period under consideration Hillary Rodham Clinton was chair of the CDF board and Donna Shalala, the current HHS secretary, was a member of the board. Shalala replaced Clinton as chair in February 1992.

49. Health Care Financing Administration, "Special Terms and Conditions," 19 March 1993. The HSC submitted its newest list to the legislature 19 April 1993. The list contains 696 condition/treatment pairs. The proposal is to make the cut-off number 565. Oregon Health Services Commission, *Prioritization of Health Services, 1993,* Appendix F.
50. Observers of the Salem scene also suggest that the tobacco lobby, which provides substantial campaign funds in the state, has become interested in the issue as well.
51. *The Oregonian,* 4 April 1993, B3.
52. Health Care Financing Administration, "Special Terms and Conditions," 2.
53. *The Oregonian,* 27 March 1993, B2.
54. D. Sarashon, "Oregon Might Just Waive the Waiver," *The Oregonian,* 21 February 1993, C2.
55. Memorandum, 26 December 1990.
56. Ibid.
57. W.H. Hedrick and L.H. Zeigler, "Oregon: The Politics of Power," in *Interest Groups in the American West,* ed. R.J. Hrebenar and C.S. Thomas (Salt Lake City: University of Utah Press, 1987), 109–110.

Health Care Reform in Vermont: A Work in Progress

Howard M. Leichter

INTRODUCTION

In the spring of 1992 a coalition of Vermont health care providers, business groups, and bipartisan political leaders joined forces to fashion the Vermont Health Care Act (Act 160). The law, if fully implemented, will assure all Vermonters access to a uniform package of health care services, control the costs of health care through a statewide global budget, reduce unfairness in health insurance through community rating, reform medical malpractice laws, and place health care policy under a single state authority.

The Vermont experience challenges the conventional wisdom concerning coalition building in the process of health care reform. For example, Vermont physicians accepted greater state involvement in some areas, such as global budgeting and practice parameters, in exchange for the promise that lengthy and costly malpractice litigation, micromanagement by government agencies, and the blizzard of paperwork required by insurance companies and government would be reduced.

In addition, many Vermont physicians, hospital administrators, business groups, and others see an essentially market-based system, with elements of managed care and/or managed competition, as far preferable to either the current system or a Canadian-style single-payer system. Finally, postponing certain difficult choices may be the political price lawmakers have to pay to begin and sustain the reform process. In the case of Vermont, for example, the state still must devise solutions to fundamental issues: What level of health care will each Vermonter receive? How will universal access be funded? Should the state adopt a market-based, multiple-payer system, a Canadian-style single-payer system, or something else?

VERMONT HEALTH CARE ACT

The Vermont Health Care Act of 1992 begins with the premise that all Vermonters should have "access to quality health services at costs which are affordable." To accomplish this the state is attempting to improve the quality of health care, reduce costs and administrative fragmentation in the system, encourage local and regional participation in health policy decisions, and promote a more rational allocation of health care resources in the state. As stipulated in the law, the reform is incremental: it began in 1992 and, if all goes according to plan, will culminate in 1994 with implementation of a universal access plan.

TABLE 1
Timetable for Reform **1992**
• The Vermont Health Care Act developed an insurance purchasing pool for employees of the state, the University of Vermont, Vermont State Colleges, municipalities, school districts, as well as some Medicaid recipients. Others may join the pool later upon approval of the General Assembly after October 1993. (As of October 1993, this provision had not yet been implemented, and state officials were of the opinion that it may need amending.) • The Act expanded the state's Dr. Dynasaur program to cover both pregnant women and low- and moderate-income children up to age 17 who do not qualify for Medicaid. (Prior to reform the program covered children from birth to age six.) Under the new law a family of four earning less than $30,150 a year is eligible for free medical care for their children. All copayments in the program have been eliminated.

- The Act created the Vermont Health Care Authority (VHCA) which is under the direction of a three-member board. The authority has begun work on a comprehensive health care database covering expenditures, utilization, and services.
- The state secretary of administration has established a so-called health insurance safety net for the following groups: (1) individuals in the nongroup or small group market who lose coverage either because their insurer withdraws from the Vermont market—something which a number of carriers threatened to do—or their insurer failed to register by 1 July 1993, as a nongroup carrier; or (2) individuals in the group market who lose their jobs and are not subsequently covered by another group plan.

1993

- The state insurance commissioner, in consultation with the VHCA, has developed mandatory uniform health insurance claims forms and standard procedures for processing claims to help reduce health care costs. Insurers submitted cost management plans to the VHCA.
- The VHCA board has adopted a Health Resource Management Plan, which evaluates health resources in the state and sets goals and priorities for their distribution.
- In July the VHCA board adopted a nonbinding health care expenditure target.
- Community rating for nongroup (i.e., individual) insurance policies will go into effect in July. This will affect the approximately 35,000 Vermonters who purchase insurance policies on their own rather than through employers. Carriers are prohibited from using such risk classification criteria as age, gender, geographic setting, prior medical condition, and type of job.
- The VHCA board must submit detailed proposals to the General Assembly, in November, for two universal access health care plans: a single-payer system and a market-based, regulated multipayer system.

1994

- The University of Vermont Medical School will submit a proposal to the legislature and the VHCA to expand training of primary care physicians to encourage rural practice.
- The General Assembly will meet in January and consider the board's proposals. Lawmakers are not bound to adopt either or any plan.
- If the legislature adopts a plan for universal access, then a medical malpractice reform will begin. Malpractice claims would be submitted to a three-member arbitration panel. The purpose of the panel is to accelerate the process of malpractice claims and thereby reduce the cost and anxiety for all parties in the procedure. The arbitration decision could be appealed to the Vermont Superior Court.
- Regardless of whether a universal access plan is adopted, the VHCA, after public hearings and negotiations with provider bargaining groups and insurers, will establish annual unified health care budgets, or global budgets, that set total spending levels on health care and are the main vehicle for controlling health care costs in Vermont. At a minimum, spending caps will be applied to hospitals.

The centerpiece of the law is the Vermont Health Care Authority (VHCA), which began its work in August 1992. The VHCA acts under the direction of an administratively powerful, three-member board appointed by the governor and confirmed by the senate. (The current board consists of a former state representative, a former state commissioner of social welfare, and a professor of economics at the University of Vermont.) The board's responsibilities are far-reaching and include program design (typically requiring legislative approval), data collection, and advisory work with other agencies involved in implementing the reform. The board also works with existing public organizations to encourage local and regional health plans and primary health care systems and to negotiate with provider groups. The board represents one of the most highly centralized and potentially powerful health care agencies in the country.

THE ROAD TO HEALTH CARE REFORM

By the time Vermonters embarked on their ambitious reform in 1992, state lawmakers, health care providers, and other key players could draw on more than a decade of shared history with state involvement in health care regulation. The antecedents of the Vermont Health Reform Act can be traced at least as far back as 1979, when the state enacted a certificate-of-need (CON) law, requiring hospitals and other health care institutions to apply to the health department for review and approval of new capital expenditures and the introduction of new health services. In 1987 this responsibility was moved to an independent, quasi-judicial CON board, and in 1990 the process was expanded to review some physician office services. It is indicative of the generally positive relationship that has existed between the state and health care providers that, contrary to the negative views and experiences of health care providers in other states, CON receives high praise in Vermont.

This relationship was taken a step further in 1983, with the creation of a Hospital Data Council. The five-member council was responsible for conducting annual budget reviews of Vermont's 18 nonprofit hospitals and making cost control recommendations. In addition, it collected and analyzed financial and utilization data provided by the hospitals. Although a recent study found that "the Council's [budget] recommendations can be, and often are, ignored," it has provided policy makers with a good database on the cost and utilization of hospital care in the state.[1]

The state's first actual foray into dealing with its uninsured population came in 1987, with the creation of the Vermont Health Insurance Plan (VHIP) board, an administrative ancestor of the VHCA. The plan was the result of a joint effort by low-income advocates and state legislators to press for universal access to health care in the state. The legislation set up a board composed of representatives of low-income people, business groups, the Vermont Medical Association, the Vermont Hospital Association, the Vermont Employers Health Alliance, the Vermont Chamber of Commerce, and the insurance industry. Thus the key institutional and individual players in health policy began working together, within the context of a state-supported enterprise, to assess health care access in the state.

The VHIP board was charged with studying ways to extend health insurance to the uninsured. The following year the board recommended a pay-or-play option for Vermont businesses, and a state subsidy to finance a basic package of health services for the state's uninsured population. An actuarial study estimated that it would cost about $30 million to provide a comprehensive benefits package to the approximately 32,000 uninsured Vermonters (just under 6 percent of the state's population). The VHIP board recommended a pay-or-play option for Vermont businesses and a state subsidy to implement the plan. Neither the Vermont General Assembly nor Governor Madeline Kunin (D) was willing to support a significant increase in state spending on health care at that time.

The 1988 legislature did, however, extend access to one portion of that uninsured population, namely, children up to age seven and women whose family incomes were above the Medicaid eligibility level but below 225 percent of the poverty level. This became the Prenatal and Children's Health Program (better known as "Dr. Dynasaur"), a highly successful and popular state effort.

Although ultimately unsuccessful in its overall goal, the VHIP program was important because it demonstrated that health care reform was no longer merely an issue for advocates of low-income people and liberal politicians. Physicians, hospital administrators, the business community, and the insurance industry were also behind demands for change. More important, all the players accepted the principle of universal access to health care. Part of the reason behind the broad response was that health care reform engaged different groups for different reasons: low-income advocates continued to emphasize access; physicians were troubled by increased governmental micromanagement of their practice and by malpractice litigation; and business leaders decried skyrocketing health insurance costs and their impact on profits and competitiveness.

Thus, by the beginning of the 1991–92 legislative session, the state had an experiential basis on which to build health reform. Moreover, indications from key organizations were clear that a major overhaul of Vermont's health care system was needed and would be supported. In fact, during the first year of the biennium detailed reform plans were introduced by several organizations, including the Vermont State Medical Society, the Vermont Hospital Association, the Vermont Employers Health Alliance, and the Vermont Consumers Campaign for Health.[2]

The most authoritative and influential of these plans was sponsored by the government itself. In March 1991 Governor Richard Snelling (R) created the Vermont Blue Ribbon Commission on Health, popularly known as the Gibb Commission after its chairman, former Republican State Senator Arthur Gibb. The commission was "to explore and design a comprehensive group of proposals," which would, among other things, ensure "access to adequate health care for all Vermonters."[3]

The 24-member Commission met between 25 March and 16 December 1991 and submitted its final report to the governor on the eve of the 1992 legislative session. The commission proposed "that universal health care should be available to all Vermont residents." The report, which was submitted to the governor in December, contained an ambitious list of recommendations, including a guarantee to all Vermonters of access to "a common set of comprehensive health care benefits," reform of the state's medical malpractice laws, state encouragement of managed care and health promotion to help control health costs, and improvements in rural health care. The commission recommended the creation of a Vermont Health Care Authority, with the responsibility to insure universal access and contain health care costs.[4]

Significantly enough, the commission's position on the insurance mechanism for a restructured state health care system adumbrated that of the 1992 reform act: it made no recommendation. As the commission admitted in its report, "This issue of single-payer versus 'single-processor' (or 'regulated-payer') system was the focus of the most profound debate which occurred in the [Cost Containment and Finance] Task Group.[5] The Task Group could not reach agreement on the best way to control health care costs: single-payer or regulated multi-payer. The group assumed a single-payer system would include prospective budgeting, global expenditure caps, and elimination of private insurance companies. Single-payer advocates, both on the committee and those who gave testimony, argued that only through these features could the state realize significant savings while achieving universal access. Those favoring a regulated multipayer system were loath to eliminate private insurance carriers, and placed their faith in market competition, public health education, and managed care to achieve cost control.

In the end, it was clear that neither position enjoyed a majority of the group and, therefore, the members decided to merely report the pros and cons of each system without the Task Group or the full commission taking a formal stand. A majority of the members believed that more analysis of the purported virtues and vices of each system were needed and that the health authority proposed by the commission would be the appropriate vehicle for conducting that analysis. The Gibb Commission's report thus prefigured the Vermont Health Care Act.

During this same period Vermont's statewide political leadership, too, weighed in on behalf of fundamental health care reform and, in particular, universal access. On 7 December 1991, Governor Howard Dean (D) (who had replaced Snelling after his death), Senators James Jeffords (R) and Patrick Leahy (D), and Representative Bernard Sanders (I) each appeared at a so-called People's Special Session on Health Care held at the State House in Montpelier. The meeting was called by a coalition favoring a legislative proposal for a Canadian-style, single-payer system in Vermont. Although all four leaders endorsed the principle of universal access, only Representative Sanders, the former socialist mayor of Burlington, supported the single-payer proposal.

Finally, the 1991 session also witnessed a significant legislative victory when the Vermont General Assembly approved Act 52, which required insurance companies to use community rating and guaranteed acceptance of clients in writing policies for the small group health insurance market. This part of the story began in the summer of 1990, when Blue Cross/Blue Shield of Vermont met with business leaders around the state to explain the financial crisis facing the state's largest insurance carrier, which had sustained losses of over $20 million between 1985 and 1990 in its nongroup insurance market. Company representatives explained that this had largely resulted from the requirement of their state charter that they use community rating and guaranteed acceptance of clients. Because they were the only insurer in the state using these practices, other carriers were able to choose the best insurance risks for coverage. Blue Cross/Blue Shield consequently had the burden of insuring the highest-risk, most costly portion of the Vermont market. Because the carrier could not continue to take such losses and stay in businesses, company officials urged that other insurance carriers be required to play by the same rules as the Blues, at least in the small-group market (businesses with fewer than 50 employees).

By the time the General Assembly convened in 1991, Governor Richard Snelling (R) and state banking and insurance commissioner Jeffrey Johnson agreed to support community rating and guaranteed acceptance throughout the small-group market. Despite insurance company warnings that many carriers would cease writing small group policies in Vermont if the bill was enacted, the legislature approved small group insurance reform (Act 52).

The importance of Act 52 can not be overstated. Legislators realized that they could take on the insurance companies, one of the most powerful forces in the health field, and win. As one lobbyist for the insurance industry explained, "Something happened in 1991. In the first place, the legislature found they could actually enact a bill with community rating. After all this labor, they'd given birth to this thing. They pinched themselves and found out the sun still came up in the morning, and it could be done."[6] The effort was additionally important because it brought together some of the key players who would reassemble for the 1992 reform act.

One player who would be missing was Governor Snelling, who died unexpectedly in August 1991. He was succeeded in office by the Democratic Lieutenant Governor Howard Dean, M.D., an internist who, until he became governor, continued to practice medicine. It is important to underscore the effect that Howard Dean's becoming governor had on the timing and tenor of the reform effort. Dr. Dean, for example, shares the distaste of his colleagues for federal micromanagement of medical practices, especially through the much despised Medicare program. "I hate micromanagement," said Dean. "My biggest fear has been . . . that the federal government would impose Medicare for everybody, and that would be national health care. And in that case I think you would see the end of decent health care in this country. I didn't want to see that in Vermont."[7]

Dean's medical background clearly influenced his political judgment on one of the most hotly contested and significant portions of the reform act, namely, community rating in the nongroup policy market. In discussing the insurance industry's opposition to community rating, Dean observed, "I've seen how these companies operate, I know what they were all about because they've insured some of my patients, and every time they had a bill [from me], they would do their best not to pay. So I was most anxious to show them the door."[8]

THE GOSPEL OF THE SINGLE-PAYER PLAN

If the emergence of Howard Dean as governor was comforting to the medical community, the appearance of another political actor in 1991 proved much less so. In 1990 Cheryl Rivers, a progressive Democrat, was elected state senator from Windsor County. Rivers had long championed the cause of Vermont's poor, serving as a lobbyist for the Vermont Low-Income Advocacy Council. As a freshman senator in 1991, Rivers was appointed to the critical Senate Health and Welfare Committee, which was chaired by Sally Conrad, with whom Rivers had worked before on the VHIP program, and who was herself an advocate of a single-payer system.

One of Rivers's first acts as senator was to introduce a bill (S. 127) that would provide universal access to a comprehensive package of health care benefits through a single-payer insurance system. Rivers and Conrad decided to use the first year of the biennium "to educate the [Senate Health and Welfare] Committee, educate other legislators, and raise the issues in the public eye."[9] As part of this process, Conrad's committee decided to study the issues over the summer of 1991. Committee members went around the state soliciting the views of various interest groups, political leaders, and administration officials.

In this effort, Rivers and Conrad were joined by two liberal Vermont political heavyweights. The first was the state branch of the National Educational Association, Vermont-NEA, with nearly 8,000 members and one of the best lobbying organizations in the state. Vermont-NEA held a series of informational meetings on the Rivers plan, and distributed 10,000 bumper stickers ("*Every* Vermonter Deserves Health Care) and 100,000 fliers ("We have a Vermont Solution to our Health Care Crisis . . . and it won't cost us any more money!") in support of S. 127. Vermont-NEA was also responsible for a "letters to the editor" campaign around the state.

The second force behind the single-payer campaign was Vermont's maverick and politically astute congressman, Bernie Sanders. Sanders, who had close ties to both Rivers and Vermont-NEA, used his considerable political skills on behalf of the single-payer idea, appearing on several occasions with Rivers at meetings and rallies in support of S. 127.

THE VERMONT HEALTH REFORM ACT: THE LEGISLATIVE PROCESS

Coalition building. Two things were clear as the state's political leadership prepared for the 1992 legislative session: there was broad and deep support for health care reform, and the option with the most visibility was S. 127. A single-payer system was, however, unacceptable to many in government and to key portions of the business community and provider industry. During the spring and summer of 1991, the single-payer advocates had done an extraordinary job stimulating and cultivating popular support for their plan and raising the anxiety level of several key players in the game. In fact, the fear that Cheryl Rivers, Sally Conrad, and other single-payer proponents might prevail was a major participating factor in Vermont's move:

> "That [single-payer group] was so vocal about their single-payer [plan], which was based totally on ideological feelings and not on fact, that the business community and the providers were terrified by it and joined up with us." (Governor Howard Dean)
>
> "But people were scared to death of these lefties out there who are roaring down this Canada road—single payer." (Former state representative Hamilton Davis)
>
> "There was universal agreement . . . among business [groups], among providers, that S. 127 as constructed would not work in Vermont, and therefore, we had to be opposed to it." (Norman Wright, President, the Vermont Hospital Association)
>
> "A member of the House said to me, 'The whole agenda here was to stop Rivers; beyond party [considerations], beyond anything.' I think that's absolutely right." (Senator Cheryl Rivers)

Some who opposed S. 127 did so on the ideological grounds that it involved too much government intervention. Others, like Howard Dean and Jeanne Keller, president of the Vermont Employers Alliance, felt that the bill was a fiscal and policy leap in the dark.

The Vermont State Medical Society had yet another reason to oppose the bill. In both its original (1991) and revised (January 1992) form, S. 127 specifically excluded health care providers from participation in the proposed health care authority. The medical society, and their member physicians, found this both troubling and offensive. As Nancy Eldridge, director of governmental relations for the Vermont State Medical Society, explained, the deliberate and pointed exclusion of providers was interpreted as a message to physicians that said, "You will not participate in this. You are the bad guys. You are the ones to be regulated. We will set your reimbursement, and if you don't like it, that's just too bad."[10]

For a variety of reasons, then, opposition to S. 127 attracted a coalition that, according to Howard Dean, was "different from any other state's coalition."[11] It included people from the business community, the hospital association, the medical society, Blue Cross/Blue Shield, as well as the Democratic speaker of the house Ralph Wright, Governor Dean, and the Republican house majority leader Sara Gear. As one player explained to me, "It was fairly easy in some ways for us to build the necessary coalition if we could find something to bind it together. There needed to be a common goal, and the common goal really was [defeat of] S. 127."[12]

In December 1991 the Democratic House Speaker, Ralph Wright, announced his intention to pursue health reform in the upcoming session. A month earlier Wright and Governor Dean had agreed to join forces in this effort. Because the state had a $57.2 million deficit, both the speaker and the governor agreed that reform would have to be gradual and not require a significant investment of new money.

Very early in the process, the Republican leadership, which had created its own task force on reform, decided to back the Dean/Wright plan. Despite partisan considerations, the Wright bill, H. 733, shared enough in common with the Gibb Commission report—which had been created by a Republican governor and chaired by a former Republican state senator—to provide common ground for substantial substantive agreement. The bill had one other important virtue: it was not a single-payer plan. The Wright bill was introduced in the House in January and, in almost unprecedented fashion, was cosponsored by the speaker, the Republican house majority and assistant majority leaders, and two assistant Democratic minority leaders.

As originally introduced, the bill provided for the establishment of a three-member health care authority that would do the following:

1. Design a health care database.
2. Adopt annual health care expenditure targets.
3. Establish a statewide health care resource management plan.
4. Conduct hospital budget reviews.
5. Administer the CON program.
6. Design a common benefits program that would constitute a minimum standard for health insurance plans offered in Vermont and "serve as the administrator and single negotiator with hospitals and providers for common benefits provided through the plan."
7. Design and implement a unified system of purchasing medical supplies and equipment.

H. 733 contained two other significant proposals. The first, building on the insurance reform of the previous legislature, proposed expanding community rating to the nongroup or individual insurance market. To some, including the governor, this provision would offer the most important immediate benefit of the act. It would also prove to be one of the most contentious issues. Nongroup community rating would make affordable health insurance more accessible to some Vermonters (e.g., older people and those with preexisting medical conditions), but more costly to others (e.g., younger, healthier people).

A second issue was malpractice reform, a matter of considerable importance to two powerful lobbies—physicians and attorneys. The legislative finding introducing the tort reform section reflected the main concerns of both physicians and plaintiffs—namely, that the system is slow, costly, inaccessible to many, and seemingly unconnected to quality assurance in medical practice.

Finally, the bill addressed the extreme administrative fragmentation of the state's current health care system by bringing various preexisting state agencies under the jurisdiction of the new health authority.

Legislative politics. The legislative odyssey of H. 733 took more than three months—January through April 1992—and involved an unusually high level of personal effort by the governor, his staff, and the legislative leadership. Governor Dean and his office carefully tracked the bill, met with committee members, helped work out compromises when the legislative process bogged down, briefed interest group leaders, and helped bring in the votes—at one point the governor literally walked the legislative lobby seeking support of the bill. Speaker Wright, too, was unusually involved. In unprecedented fashion, he sat in on committee meetings, hand carried the bill from the Commerce Committee to the Health and Welfare Committee, and gave the Appropriations Committee just 30 minutes to debate and vote on it. Despite all this effort, the bill's legislative voyage was not at all smooth.

Problems began in the House of Representatives, where H. 733 had initially been assigned to the Health and Welfare Committee. However, a jurisdictional and personal problem emerged between the Health and Welfare and the Commerce committees. The chairman of the Commerce Committee was Paul Harrington (R), a highly regarded legislator with considerable experience in insurance reform—his committee had crafted Act 52 the previous year. Harrington believed that H. 733 was poorly drafted and wanted a more active role in revising the bill than would be the case if the Health and Welfare Committee retained dominant jurisdiction. An agreement was worked out whereby the Health and Welfare Committee released the bill to Commerce, which gave it full scrutiny. Harrington, along with Peg Martin, the chairperson of Health and Welfare, and Claudia Bristow, a member of the Legislative Counsel's Office, redrafted the bill that was ultimately approved by key legislative leaders and the governor.

With a redraft in its possession and greater autonomy over its content, the Commerce Committee, much to the annoyance of its colleagues on Health and Welfare, proceeded to address all aspects of the bill. The result was several weeks of sometimes strained exchanges between the two committees (actually three additional committees, because Judiciary, Appropriations, and Government Operations looked at the bill as well), as each held public hearings and brought different perspectives to the task.

The strain was in part about protecting legislative turf and in part about substantive disagreements. The policy differences ranged from the trivial, such as the salaries and length of terms of the health authority members, to the more consequential. For example, the Health and Welfare Committee favored limiting participation in the insurance purchasing pool to health benefit plans funded in whole or in part by state funds, whereas the Commerce Committee proposed beginning the pool with public employees, but eventually extending it to private individuals and groups. Further, although Commerce wanted to require community rating in the pool, Health and Welfare did not.[13]

Because of these intramural disputes, Speaker Wright took the unprecedented step of sitting in on committee meetings in order to help shepherd his bill through the process. As a practical matter, the bill had to clear the House within six to eight weeks so that the Senate would have an equal amount of time to consider it. Because of the unusually large number (five) of committees dealing with the bill, and the problems between the Commerce and the Health and Welfare Committees, Wright worried that the bill would be "debated and debated to death."[14]

Fortunately, a solution to what might well have been an ugly battle presented itself just five weeks into the legislative session. At Harrington's suggestion, Speaker Wright offered Senators Conrad and Rivers a deal: they would abandon S. 127, allow H. 733 to pass through Senate Health and Welfare, and not insist on specifying a funding mechanism for any reform bill (Rivers's bill proposed a payroll tax). In return Wright would offer certain concessions, including (1) a requirement in the law that the health care authority report back to the legislature with *two* universal health plans, one a single-payer, the other a regulated multipayer, and accelerate this report from 1995 (the date proposed by the governor) to 1994; and (2) postponement of medical malpractice reform until universal access to health care was achieved. Single-payer advocates believed that the proper emphasis of reform was the consumer, not physicians; hence, the providers should receive no benefits from reform before the consumers did. Rivers and Conrad agreed immediately to the terms of the compromise, without consulting with their allies outside the legislature.

Rivers's and Conrad's agreement was the source of endless speculation and comment. Rivers later admitted that she was incredibly naive and made a mistake by not consulting with the coalition that had worked so hard, and supported her for so long, on the single-payer plan. According to Rivers, "In retrospect, I wish I had said to Ralph, 'I've gotta have a couple of days to go back and talk to people.' But it happened too fast and they weren't part of the process. That hurt a lot. That was a mistake."[15]

Why did Rivers and Conrad abandon their plan so quickly? Why did Speaker Wright make concessions to the two senators? In answer to the first question, all the players, including Senators Conrad and Rivers and the speaker, agree that S. 127 did not have enough votes to get out of the Senate Health and Welfare Committee, much less through the General Assembly. Although there may have been strong popular support for a single-payer plan, there was relatively little legislative enthusiasm for it. A January 1992 survey by the *Burlington Free Press* found that only about one-third of the legislators favored a single-payer system.[16] Moreover, this support eroded in January, when Senator John Carroll (R), an opponent of the single-player plan and the author of a Republican alternative for health reform, released a study by the legislative joint fiscal office. The study showed that Rivers's financing plan would fall far short of the revenue needed to pay for her program. Rivers, who contested the report's findings, admitted, "That scored a pretty direct hit. At this point it had become clear to me that whether the cost [predicted by the fiscal office] was right or wrong, we couldn't have modified my bill to say, 'We're going to set up a health care authority, and it's supposed to design a single-payer system, and cost it out and come back next January with the figures.'"[17] The credibility of the Rivers plan, at least among her colleagues, was irreparably damaged.

If a single-payer could not pass, why bother making concessions? There are a number of possible explanations. First, although there was little support for S. 127 inside the state house, there was considerable popular support. According to Representative Hamilton Davis (D), a member of the Health and Welfare Committee, "Ralph knows there's a lot of heat out there. He's reading the same newspapers everybody else is reading. He can see that it would be highly desirable in political process terms [to reach an accommodation]. . . . A lot of his guys are saying 'Ralph, I'm with you all the way, but when I went home yesterday and it was just me and 90 people there, 89 of them said, 'How come you're not supporting single payer?' "[18]

A second explanation lies in the speaker's politics. A political pragmatist, Wright knew what he wanted in health care reform: universal access to a comprehensive benefits package and a plan that was fiscally realistic and sound. He was neither committed, nor opposed, to any particular vision of health reform, although he believes that a multipayer system is politically more practical. As he later acknowledged, "Quite frankly my input into the bill after the initial draft was much less than a number of other people."[19] This view is shared by Wright's colleagues. Again, Representative Davis: "To Ralph, the main thing is to get a bill that is going to do the job. The details don't matter that much."[20] The concessions he made to Conrad and Rivers were far less important than the removal of an obstacle to reform.

A third explanation for the speaker's intervention is that he was helping out a governor of his own party. The legislation taking place involved a number of partners. Howard Dean and his staff were working closely with the legislature to build a consensus around H. 733. From their perspective, Rivers and Conrad continued to pose a threat to the reform because they showed no signs of abandoning their single-payer crusade. Furthermore, relations between the governor and the two senators were not especially good at the time. At this point the speaker decided to explain the political facts of life to his colleagues from the other chamber: they did not have the votes for their own bill, and they had to decide whether they wanted to be viewed as obstructionist to or supportive of reform.

With the deal, a major impediment to passage of H. 733 was removed—

so it seemed. The single-payer plan was dead, at least for this session; but Sally Conrad and Cheryl Rivers were still very much alive. Their main concession was to concede the political battlefield to H. 733; they did not abandon their right to try and change that bill once it got to the Senate.

On 21 February, about six weeks after it was first introduced in committee, the House Health and Welfare Committee voted unanimously to recommend H. 733 to the full House. The major provisions of the committee bill, which for the most part were adopted by the full House, included the creation of a Health Care Authority; development of two plans for universal access to health care; mechanisms for cost control, including hospital budget reviews, a health care management plan, global budgeting, utilization review procedures, uniform health insurance forms and claims procedures; a health insurance purchasing pool; community rating of the nongroup market; and medical malpractice reform. The House approved the measure a week later by a vote of 119 to 17.

H. 733 now entered the much less friendly arena of the Vermont Senate, where the progressives enjoyed greater strength and the bill would be taken up by Senator Conrad's Health and Welfare Committee. Depending on who you listen to, the five-member Senate Health and Welfare committee, with two progressive Democrats (Conrad and Rivers) and one staunch conservative Republican either "eviscerated" the bill or "improved" it.[21]

The critical moment in the process came on 10 March, when the Senate Health and Welfare committee voted (3–2) to strip H. 733 of the insurance purchasing pool, community rating, and medical malpractice reform. The result was explosive. As Cheryl Rivers described it, "Once we took those sections out of the bill, all hell broke loose."[22] Jeanne Keller, president of the Vermont Employers Health Alliance, said of Conrad and Rivers, "It seems that if they can't get universal access right now and under their terms, they'll kill any effort to improve the lot of Vermonters, even temporarily."[23]

Conrad and Rivers had several objections to H. 733. First, it did not immediately address the needs of the state's approximately 60,000 people who were uninsured. Second, they were concerned that community rating would drive insurers from the state, leaving thousands of Vermonters without coverage or alternative carriers (many insurance companies were threatening to leave). Third, insurers warned that many Vermonters would face "rate shock" when community rating went into effect. This would happen to the younger and healthier Vermonters, who would subsidize the decreased premiums that older, sicker persons would be paying under the community rating and guaranteed acceptance provisions of the legislation. Many in the legislature, including the two senators, were hearing from constituents who were being alerted to this danger by their insurance companies.

Conrad and Rivers argued that the insurance pool, while negotiating favorable rates for its members (e.g., state employees), would cause rate increases for nonpool subscribers as insurance companies made up for lost revenues in that market. The result, they argued, would be that some would be forced to drop their policies and join the ranks of the uninsured. Finally, Conrad and Rivers had never reconciled themselves to medical malpractice reform, even after their compromise with the speaker to postpone its implementation until after a universal access plan was in place.

Ultimately a compromise was worked out between the governor's staff and the two senators. It provided for the following:

- The creation of an insurance safety net to protect individuals who lose their insurance because their insurer has pulled out of the Vermont market. This service would be provided by a nonprofit hospital and medical service corporation.

- To avoid increased rates the Commissioner of Banking, Insurance, and Securities would set maximum annual premium percentage rate increases. Under no circumstances could the commissioner approve a rate increase greater than 20 percent in any year. In addition, the insurance commissioner was granted the authority to deny a rate increase for any nongroup insurance policy in which the insurer paid out less than 70 percent of the premiums in claims in the previous year.[24]
- The establishment of a Vermont Health Care Purchasing Pool Trust Fund under the Secretary of Administration. The secretary was authorized to withdraw funds from the pool to subsidize the purchase of health care services for uninsured Vermonters on an income-based, sliding-fee scale.
- Health care benefits under the Dr. Dynasaur program for non-Medicaid-eligible children and pregnant women will be extended up to age 18 from its current limit of age 6. In addition, current copayments in program will be eliminated.
- The state would allocate $350,000 to the University of Vermont College of Medicine to fund six additional family practice residency positions.
- Malpractice reform remained unresolved. Each side agreed to take its case to the full Senate.

Both sides expressed satisfaction with the deal, and the bill was approved in Health and Welfare. However, H. 733 was not yet home free; it still had to be considered by both the Senate Finance and Judiciary Committees. Although the bill narrowly passed the Finance Committee, committee members were concerned about the safety net and the bill's seemingly hostile attitude to commercial insurers. Interestingly enough, the main opponent in Finance was Senator John Carroll (R), who had provided the coup de grace on single-payer insurance and who had been a supporter of H. 733, but who apparently had second thoughts about the community rating provision of the bill.

Another problem occurred in the Senate Judiciary Committee, where the state's Bar and Trial Lawyers associations successfully lobbied to prohibit admission of the malpractice arbitration board's findings in a jury trial. The lawyers argued that jurors should not be exposed to any nonjudicial decisions that might influence their judgment. At this point the Vermont State Medical Society threatened to withdraw its support if the committee's decision was not reversed. Nevertheless, the Judiciary Committee approved the change and sent it on to the full Senate. The Dean administration and speaker Ralph Wright were clearly troubled by this turn of events and by the possible defection of the medical society.

The bill's next test came in the full Senate. Insurance companies, which had unsuccessfully fought to remove the community rating provision, marshaled their forces for one last assault. The insurance industry, however, had few friends in the Senate, and that body easily defeated an effort to remove community rating. Next, the senators overrode their Judiciary Committee colleagues and voted to admit an arbitration panel's decision as evidence in a jury trial. On 13 April the Senate passed H. 733 by a vote of 23 to 4.

It now remained for the House and Senate to iron out the nearly 30, mostly minor, differences between the two measures. The conference lasted several days, and from all reports achieving compromise was quite difficult. According to Peg Martin, one of the conferees, "My main memory of the conference committee was the acrimony of it all. It was a very, very disagreeable . . . experience."[25] Indeed, at one particularly tense moment, the House conferees

(Representatives Hamilton Davis, Paul Harrington, and Peg Martin) walked out, threatening not to return. Some of the discord resulted from clashing personalities; some, from different institutional and ideological perspectives. In retrospect several of the most contentious issues, such as the proposed starting dates for various provisions, or whether the VHCA could begin its work before receiving formal Senate confirmation, were irrelevant to the main goals of the reform. In the heated atmosphere of the conference, however, they took on important symbolic significance.

In fact, there were only a few real differences. One was participation in the insurance purchasing pool. The House version prohibited private employee groups or individuals from joining the pool; the Senate favored opening the pool. Jeffrey Johnson, the state banking and insurance commissioner, explained the real issue: "There was a lot of concern that the pool could be used as the Trojan horse of health care reform. And, frankly, that's not a completely wrong thought. The pool, if it's big enough, can ultimately become a very large player in deciding how health care is administered in the State of Vermont, particularly in a state of 500,000 people if it ends up with 100,000 risks."[26] In the end the Senate conferees prevailed, although the legislature must approve the admission of private groups or individuals to the pool. (As of this writing the status of the purchasing pool is still very much undecided.)

A second issue involved the definition of single-payer and multipayer systems. The House wanted to leave the definitions open, allowing the VHCA maximum flexibility. The Senate on the other hand wanted detailed definitions to prevent any bias the authority might have toward a particular plan. In the Senate version, which was ultimately adopted, the single-payer system was modeled after the Canadian system and the multipayer plan after the German model.

Finally, the two houses differed over two provisions that would address specific problems in delivering health care. The first was expansion of the Dr. Dynasaur program. The House was concerned about the financial effect of expanding the program (at a cost of $750,000) when the state was running a huge deficit, although they ultimately accepted the expansion. Second, the House opposed the Senate-inspired provision requiring the University of Vermont Medical School to add four family practice residencies. The House conferees argued that this interfered with the professional judgment of the institution; their view prevailed. At this point the conference report went back to each house, where it was approved overwhelmingly.

The role of interest groups. The activity of interest groups throughout the legislative process was intense. To supporters of a single-payer system, such as Vermont-NEA, the critical juncture was the Wright-Rivers-Conrad summit in February. From then on, their efforts were not nearly as intense or enthusiastic as they had been before 7 February, although they did continue to monitor the process. For example, no one from Vermont-NEA, which had invested heavily in S. 127, formally testified before any legislative committee on H. 733, although they did not actively oppose the bill and, in fact, enthusiastically endorsed some of its provisions (e.g., expansion of the Dr. Dynasaur program).

Some viewed the demise of S. 127 with deep regret; others were delighted. The Vermont State Medical Society (VSMS), for example, left no doubt where it stood on the two measures: "The two bills which are the subject of most discussions are H. 733 and S. 127. We have major concerns with S. 127, whereas our concerns and questions regarding H. 733 may be resolvable."[27] The society's lobbyists appeared at least once and often several times before each legislative committee. In addition, the VSMS set up a statewide "Key Contact

Network," which consisted of volunteers whom their colleagues could contact about the bill. The society sent physicians periodic "alerts," which asked them to contact their representatives directly and express support or opposition to particular provisions of H. 733.

As noted earlier, Vermont physicians were, in the first instance, concerned that they not be cast as the heavies and excluded from the process of reform—precisely the role they felt was allocated to them under S. 127. The VSMS wanted physician participation in the various councils, panels and boards envisioned in H. 733. In this way doctors could influence rules governing practice parameters, compensation rates and contracts, the health care budget, and benefits package.

Another major concern of the profession was malpractice reform. Physician support for arbitration appeared to be based less on determining the size of rewards and more on accelerating the lengthy, and emotionally debilitating, litigation process. The arbitration process promised, indeed mandated, quicker resolution (e.g., within three months) resolution of malpractice claims. In the end, despite considerable anxiety and uncertainty about what the future might hold once the Authority came in with its funding proposal, the VSMS declared itself "very happy with the final bill."[28]

The Vermont Hospital Association, too, supported the general direction of H. 733. However, it had specific objections to the bill as it underwent its various transformations in committee. Much like their colleagues in the medical society, with whom they worked closely throughout this process, the hospital association was particularly concerned that cost-containment measures did not occur largely in the form of unreasonable hospital budget caps. The association felt this was particularly unfair because its member hospitals had voluntarily imposed limits on net patient care revenues in fiscal years 1992 and

1993, and it expressed this view in March to Governor Dean. They were generally pleased with the outcome, but they believe that 1994 will be the critical year for testing their continued support.

Yet another group that declared itself "*extremely pleased with the shape of the final bill*" was the Vermont Employers Health Alliance, which stated it "*believes that Vermont is now on a sensible course toward fundamental reform of our health care financing and delivery system*" [emphasis in original].[29] Throughout the process the alliance had insisted that for reform to work it had to involve an integrated delivery and financing system, one that would help rein in health care costs. The business community supported adoption of a unified health care budget, global budgeting, a health resource management plan, and a database to help guide the authority in a rational allocation of capital and human resources and common insurance claims forms and procedures.

Although providers and business groups were generally pleased with H. 733, the insurance industry was not. With few exceptions (e.g., Blue Cross/Blue Shield), insurers saw the legislation, and especially the nongroup community rating provision, as another, perhaps fatal, assault on their profitability and autonomy. And no group played a more visible role, attracted more adverse attention, and garnered more enmity than the insurance companies. The insurance industry had suffered a major defeat the previous year with the passage of Act 52, the small group community rating law. Now they faced the prospect of losing effective underwriting control in another key market.

The insurance industry's strategy was to emphasize the harm that community rating would cause many, especially younger, Vermonters. Lobbyists from both the Health Insurance Association of America (HIAA) and individual insurance companies appeared before several legislative committees to argue that community rating would dramatically increase the premiums of younger policy holders. By one estimate, persons 24 to 25 years old could expect to see their quarterly premiums increase 303 percent, from $102.77 to $414.10. This raise would force thousands of Vermonters into the ranks of the uninsured.[30]

Although interest in their policy holders' well-being was part of the industry's concern, so too were corporate profits. Insurance companies' loss ratios, that is, how much they paid out in claims relative to the premiums they collected, were in no small measure a function of their underwriting practices. (The overall loss ratio for the ten carriers in Vermont writing nongroup policies was just under 50 percent, compared with 158 percent for Blue Cross/Blue Shield.) Writing policies for younger, healthier clients who, for example, work in law firms is more profitable than writing policies for older people with a history of medical problems, who may work in lead battery plants. The industry left little doubt what they would do if community rating was approved: "[T]here is a high probability that many of the carriers that are in Vermont now will not be in Vermont [next year] to sell policies."[31]

The bill's final version addressed many of the constituent and legislative concerns over community rating and guaranteed acceptance. Not only did the bill provide a safety net in the event that some insurers left Vermont, it also limited annual premium rate increases to no more than 20 percent. Furthermore, to qualify for a rate increase insurers had to have loss ratios of at least 70 percent.

CONCLUSION

Where, then, does Vermont stand in its pursuit of health care reform? With the exception of the formation of an insurance purchasing pool, the VHCA is on schedule for accomplishing all the tasks outlined in Table 1. Two critical chores currently occupy the authority: preparation of the two financing models and definition of a basic benefits package.

In April 1993 the Authority issued a working document that reflected current thinking on these all-important issues. According to the VHCA the goals of the reform process were to improve access, quality of care, and the health status of Vermonters while assuring provider choice and containing costs.[32] The Authority believes that these goals can best be achieved through "integrated systems of care" (ISC), which they define as "a network of providers, facilities, and administrators which has been established under a single management structure for the explicit purpose of providing a range of health care services for Vermonters." Each health care provider would join an ISC, and each Vermonter would receive health care services from an ISC of his or her choice. Although the draft document does not address the issue, presumably this system could be established within the context of either a single- or multiple-payer framework.

The other critical task of the Authority is to propose to the legislature a "Vermont Uniform Benefit Plan" that would constitute the guaranteed package of health services for all Vermonters. This task promises to be challenging for two reasons. First, as Oregonians can attest, defining a basic benefit package is a political minefield. Second, the richness of that package will define the state's cost and test the resolve and resources of state officials and state government. Clearly, a package that was inadequate would undermine the fundamental goals of the law and face opposition from many fronts, whereas a rich package might be beyond the state's capacity to fund unless it is willing to raise additional taxes.

Whatever the fate of these two issues, state officials are convinced that their reform is already or soon will be a significant accomplishment. The state will have expanded state-funded health care to include all poor and moderate-income children from birth through age 17; moreover, it has developed a global health care budget and health resources management plan, uniform health insurance claims forms, community rating throughout its insurance market, and a rationalized public health bureaucracy.

What lessons does the Vermont experience offer the rest of the nation? There is a temptation to suggest that Vermont is unique—a point Vermonters make repeatedly—so that few other states can replicate the successful coalition building there. The state is small (it has a population of 560,000 people), and there was a "friends and neighbors" approach throughout the health care debate that would have been impossible in many larger states. Add to this the fact that the state has a completely nonprofit hospital system, a physician-governor, and a medical community long supportive of state intervention in health care, and the case for uniqueness appears strong.

Nevertheless, there are lessons here that transcend Vermont's claim that it is a special case. First, the author's experiences in Oregon and Minnesota confirm the effectiveness of the "it could be a lot worse" strategy of coalition building. Fear of a Canadian-style single-payer system can bring even the most reluctant player to the table. Second, Vermont physicians have something important to say to their colleagues in other parts of the country: more government involvement in health care may mean less involvement in their practices or at least less onerous forms of involvement. The litany of complaints by Vermont physicians will be familiar to any physician in this country: They are being driven to distraction by federal micromanagement of their practices, the burden of paperwork from insurance companies, and the haunting specter of malpractice litigation. Any state-sponsored reform that promises relief from these burdens may well be embraced with enthusiasm by the provider community, especially if they are allowed to be active participants in both the formulation and implementation of policy.

Physicians, hospitals, insurance companies, and political leaders of both parties no longer question the need or likelihood of reforming the nation's health care system. The discussion is now focusing on how to achieve reform in such a way that will maximize its prospects for success. Vermont has a good deal to say to the nation on this score.

NOTES

1. "Health Care Planning and Regulation in Vermont," A Report by the Legislative Council and Joint Fiscal Office, January 1992: 19.
2. Among the various formal statements on the subject were the Vermont State Medical Society's *A Call for Health Care Reform*, the Vermont Hospital Association's *A Yardstick to Measure Health Care Reform*, and the Vermont Employers Health Alliance's *Elements of Health System Reform: An Employer Perspective*. Each of these documents included an endorsement of universal access to health care. Typical of these was the statement by the Vermont Hospital Association, "Health care is a right and no Vermonter should be denied access to care because of an inability to pay for it."
3. *Final Report of the Vermont Blue Ribbon Commission on Health,* January 1992: 2.
4. *Final Report of the Vermont Blue Ribbon Commission on Health,* January 1992.
5. The commission divided into four task groups, each of which prepared material for the plenary sessions. The four groups were Public Education and Prevention, Tort Reform, Common (Basic) Benefits, and Cost Containment and Finance.
6. Author's interview with Richard Saudek, lobbyist for the Health Insurance Association of America, 24 July 1992.
7. Author's interview with Governor Howard Dean, 21 July 1992, hereafter referred to as the Dean interview. Compare Dean's comments with those of Nancy Eldridge, Director of Governmental Relations, Vermont State Medical Society: "Our experience has been that Medicare is a horrible program. The hassle factor, and the micromanagement and. . . Medicare and the federal government and HCFA really make the physician feel like a criminal." Author's interview with Nancy Eldridge, 23 July 1992.

8. Dean interview. Dean also drew on his clinical experience when he made his State of the State address comments on health insurance in 1992. "In my own medical practice in the last two years, I have seen patients with insurance who have been fearful that they could not pay for their care. Having a deductible of $1,000 for a worker who is earning $16,000 per year is almost the same as having no health insurance at all." *Burlington Free Press*, 8 January 1992.
9. Author's interview with Senator Cheryl Rivers, 22 July 1992, hereafter referred to as the Rivers interview.
10. Author's interview with Nancy Eldridge, Director of Governmental Relations, Vermont State Medical Society, 23 July 1992, hereafter referred to as the Eldridge interview.
11. Dean interview.
12. Author's interview with Norman Wright, 21 July 1992, hereafter referred to as the Wright interview.
13. For a provision-by-provision comparison of the committee drafts, see "Memorandum from Herbert W. Olson, Legislative Counsel, to Members of the House Commerce Committee," 25 February 1992.
14. Wright interview.
15. Rivers interview.
16. *Burlington Free Press*, 5 January 1992.
17. Rivers interview.
18. Author's interview with Representative Hamilton Davis, 24 July 1992, hereafter referred to as the Davis interview.
19. Wright interview.
20. Davis interview.

21. Bryan Pfeiffer, "House-Senate Split on Health Care Widens," *Rutland Daily Herald*, 23 March 1992.
22. Rivers interview.
23. Pfeiffer, "House Senate Split on Health Care Widens."
24. A major source of antagonism toward insurance companies in Vermont was that on average the ten largest insurance companies doing business there were spending only 52 cents on medical claims for every dollar they collected; one company paid only 36 cents per dollar. By way of contrast, Blue Cross/Blue Shield paid between 85 and 90 cents for every dollar collected. The technical term for the relationship between income from premiums and payment of benefits is "loss ratio." See *Burlington Free Press*, 6 April 1992.
25. Author's interview with Representative Margaret (Peg) Martin, July 1992.
26. Author's interview with Jeffrey Johnson, Commissioner of Banking, Insurance and Securities, 27 July 1992.
27. Vermont State Medical Society. *Legislative Bulletin* 1 (24 January 1992) .
28. Eldridge interview.
29. Vermont Employers Health Alliance, "Health System Reform." (29 April 1992): 1.
30. Testimony of Suzanne Katt, Golden Rule Insurance Company, House Commerce Committee, 24 January 1992.
31. Testimony of Mark Litow, House Commerce Committee, 24 January 1992.
32. Vermont Health Care Authority, "Introduction to Integrated Systems of Care: Working Document Draft 2." 16 April 1993.